EL MAESTRO

Lady Goatherder 2

DIANE ELLIOTT

Ant Press
Large Print
Edition

Copyright © 2024 by Diane Elliott

Photographs property of Diane Elliott

Formatted and published by Ant Press

Paperback Edition ISBN: 978-1-922476-64-7

Hardback Edition ISBN: 978-1922476-67-8

Large Print Edition ISBN: 978-1-922476-68-5

Large Print Hardback Edition ISBN: 978-1-922476-69-2

All rights reserved.

Please note that this book is the original creation of the author. The author wrote and compiled it entirely without the use of any artificial intelligence.

USE OF THIS BOOK FOR AI TRAINING:

Without in any way limiting the author's and publisher's exclusive rights under copyright, any use of this publication to "train" generative artificial intelligence (AI) technologies to generate text is expressly prohibited. The author reserves all rights to license uses of this work for generative AI training and development of machine learning language models.

No part of this book may be reproduced in any form or by any electronic or mechanical means, including information storage and retrieval systems, without written permission from the author, except for the use of brief quotations in a book review.

LARGE PRINT EDITION

Contents

1. Lessons — 5
2. Martin — 23
3. Katy — 37
4. Blanquita and Bailey — 47
5. Bridge crossing at midnight — 67
6. Pups — 81
7. Rita Mae — 99
8. Medical Emergencies — 115
9. Cleft palates and cliffs — 131
10. Fast responses — 147
11. A trek — 161
12. Salado — 175
13. Flash floods and Philip — 189
14. Jonathan — 207
15. Drama in Salado — 225
16. A shock and a battle — 241
17. Roger — 253
18. Wilfs — 269
19. El Maestro — 281
20. Goats and Eagles — 295
    So, what happened next? — 315

A Request	320
About the Author	321
Acknowledgements	323
More Ant Press Books	325
Publish with Ant Press	329

1

Lessons

"Peter, Peter, look at those heels," I whisper to my husband.

A middle-aged woman is making a valiant attempt to walk up a very steep hill in four-inch stiletto heels.

"Stop staring, Diane, it's bloody rude," Peter hisses back at me, but follows my stare. The wind is blowing hard and the struggle is real.

"She won't make it up to the top," I say.

"It's coming back down that will put her in an ambulance," Peter whispers back.

I continue to gaze at the woman's heels until Peter tugs at my coat sleeve.

"For God's sake, Diane, just stop. It's not the 'done' thing. Get a grip, will you?"

I'm not sure what the 'done' thing is at a

Spanish funeral, because this is our first. I continue to look around, searching for clues. The long line of people walking behind us have their heads down, arms swinging, determined to walk up this steep road leading to the church without outwardly showing total exhaustion. I try to follow suit but am hampered by my boots. One has a hole in the sole and the other a large slit.

Light rain began to fall just as we were leaving the farm. I dash back to the kitchen and remove my boots. I find two plastic bags and pull one over each foot, then carefully shove the boots back on.

Sadly, this waterproofing plan fails halfway up the climb. The bags slide down and form a ball under both feet. This tall English lady looks as though she is walking on springs. I start to get the giggles and Peter panics.

I have been known in the past to laugh, snort and giggle at the most inappropriate times. It's probably nerves, a defence that members of my family often use to excuse me and themselves. A good example of this was at my sister's wedding.

It was a small affair, both bride and groom having been married before, and only a few friends and immediate family attended. As vows were being exchanged, my soon-to-be new brother-in-law, a prankster at the best of times, said solemnly, "I, Raymond Everett…" proudly declaring his middle name.

He then turned and stared at me. I convulsed, my nephew convulsed and then my sister followed suit. Sandra, my big sister, always calm and dignified, lost the plot at that moment and halted the ceremony… twice!

My family had not learned the lesson that I am a walking disaster on occasions that only required gentle nods accompanied by wide smiles. Or solemn nods followed by a lowering of the eyes.

My cousin insisted that I attend her wedding. She ignored my excuses that my new baby might cry and I would have to breastfeed her during the ceremony. The registrar began her welcoming chat, and baby Amelia began to cry. I discreetly shoved her head under my blouse for her to 'latch on'. She drank, then farted and had a follow through. The pong quickly permeated the small registry office. I slipped out of a side door, but apparently my hysterical laughter could be heard all the way from the car park.

Whether it's a school exam room, Doctor's waiting room, nativity play, wedding or funeral, I let the side down.

We are nearly at the top of the road and the magnificent Catholic Church stands in front of us. My boots begin to squeak.

"Antonio will find this hilarious," I say, turning to Peter.

My husband now looks really concerned. We have a long service to get through, and he now doubts his ability to curb his wife's hysteria.

"Look, Diane," Peter gently whispers. "The sun is coming out over the hills."

It's the end of March, a month that can give you four seasons in one day. Today it started off raining, then got windy and cold. As I look away from the church to Antonio's hills in the distance, the sun is starting to kiss the top ridge. If the river is low enough, I will walk the girls there this afternoon. Good grazing.

※ ※ ※

Autumn in Andalucia is welcomed with open arms. The relentless heat of a Spanish summer takes its toll on goatherders and their animals. The gentle breeze in the afternoons allowed my friend and neighbour, Antonio, and I to walk our goats high into the hills in search of fresh grazing.

It also allowed us to sit and eat a late lunch without being attacked by a billion flies or my dear friend, Alice, the most cantankerous goat in the herd. Alice had sniffed out a carob tree and had set off at high speed to devour as many pods as she could before the rest of the herd caught up.

Antonio and I sat down at the very top of the hill and ate in companionable silence. The previous two hours had been spent arguing over which goat would be the first to give birth in late November. Two hundred goats were pregnant, and during the next few months, we needed to ensure the girls had the best food on offer.

We relaxed when we could because birthing time meant little sleep and having to eat on the run. In the distance, we could see the town of Olvera, its church and castle standing guard over the surrounding white-washed houses. I tried to spear a sardine from its small tin using my pocket knife, when the church bells chimed dolefully. A funeral was in progress.

"That's Old Pedro," said Antonio, scooping a sardine with a dexterity that left me in awe.

"Oh, how sad. Was he old?" I gave up on my knife and yanked the sardine out with my fingers.

"The clue, Lady Dee, is in his name." He handed me a piece of bread to help with my ongoing sardine problem.

We sat in silence, listening to the melancholic bells. Then Antonio broke into a rant.

"It's a big con," he said.

"What's a con?" I mentally braced myself.

"Well, Pedro was about ninety years old, right?"

"Errr, right." In fact I knew nothing about the poor old chap or where this rant was going. I prayed I could keep up.

"Right. So all his friends are about the same age." He stared at me waiting for a response.

"Well, yes, I expect they are."

"Exactly. So they all have to walk up the steep hill to the church, behind the hearse." He paused for dramatic effect, taking a puff from his roll-up. "Now do you see the scam?"

"No, I don't see. What are you talking about?"

"Old people walking up a steep hill before walking back down again. That's the con." He began to shake his head, not understanding why I couldn't keep up with his train of thought. "The undertakers are rubbing their hands with glee and sizing up their next client. Why not hire a bus so that the oldies can ride up to the church? No, that is not profitable. Make them walk and money in the bank is guaranteed!"

I looked around to make sure the herd was still close by before pondering Antonio's theory. I had to admit he was probably on to something. Now it was my turn to mess with his brain.

"So, Antonio, just for argument's sake, let's say you believe in reincarnation. What animal would you come back as? Would it be a goat?"

"Me a goat! No, no. I will come back as an imperial eagle. What about you?"

"That's easy. I'll come back as my sister's cat. Central heating, lovely food, soft beds, it would be like heaven."

"A cat! A cat!" he said. "You would come back as a CAT?"

"My sister's cat. Only my sister's cat. But for heaven's sake, Antonio, you want to be an eagle but you won't even go on a plane! Where is the logic?"

That quizzical stare came back at me again. The look I had become so accustomed to. The look that said: you are a complete idiot.

"Because, Diane, I would actually be an eagle."

It was time to move the goats on. Alice had dashed back to see if Antonio had saved her an orange. Carmen the sheep, 'baa'd' the alarm. The goats were disappearing onto the next hill. Antonio took off at a fast pace to get in front of the herd, leaving me to bring up the rear.

I pondered on Antonio's reaction to me wanting to come back in my next life as a cat. I should be planning tonight's meal, but this was a better distraction than working out a magical mouth-watering recipe with two sausages, cabbage and rice.

Antonio loves cats. If he could, he would take all the stray cats that are dumped in the *campo*.

"But the dogs would murder them in ten seconds," he said once.

He took pleasure in trying to win over my old English cat, Jake, by popping down for a hot chocolate and hand-feeding my old boy bits of chicken.

Jake liked to spend time curled around my neck while I cooked or made tea. The tabby graciously accepted Antonio's offering by holding out his paw for the food. The goatherder found this amusing. This lady goatherder found it messy because bits of food fell down my neck, or ended up in my hair. He made an observation that Jake was not just a cute cat, he was Monty's mentor. Monty is my Spanish mastin.

When Rafael, the now retired goatherder from downriver, delivered a gangly black-and-tan Spanish mastin to us after we had been robbed, I had no idea how to train the young pup. In my past life I had German Shepherds and obedience-trained them. My dogs had been rejects from the Metropolitan Police. Buck, my amazing boy, may not have liked gunfire, but he turned into a fantastic tracking dog.

But I had no idea how to train a Spanish mastin. Should I use the same techniques on Monty? Antonio assured me that Monty would not need my English training tricks and that Monty would guard the girls, and me, naturally.

"Just show him the boundary of the land," he said. "Walk with him."

All of this I did, but added recall and 'wait'. He was a young pup and he also needed to play and let off steam, and so Pete found a ball. Bounce, bounce, bounce, head, toe, kick. Monty tried to copy his human dad, but his coordination was a tad off. He tripped and missed and when he finally bounced the ball, it hit him in the face.

Jake was sunbathing on the solitary deck chair that he had recently commandeered. He lazily watched the pup try to copy the human who, in turn, was trying to copy footballer George Best. Pete, sweating and puffing, took a break and joined me under the shade to glug a glass of orange juice.

We watched Monty try to pad the ball from paw to paw. Jake had seen enough. He uncurled himself from the chair and walked slowly up to the mastin pup. Monty now had the ball held firmly between his paws and was poking it with his long nose, hoping for some sort of reaction from the bouncy thing. It was a moment later that we saw real skill.

Jake's paw flashed out at the ball, stealing it, quite literally, from right under Monty's nose. He then bounced it from side to side, hit it against the wall of the house, jumped up into the air, and body-checked it before bouncing it again from paw to paw. Then Jake stopped, held the ball under his paw for a few seconds and pushed it towards Monty. He turned, jumped back onto his deck chair and fell asleep.

"Did you see that?" I whispered to Pete.

"Of course I saw that," he said. "I'm sitting right next to you. Why didn't you take photos?"

"Why didn't you get the camera?"

We fell silent as this exchange could escalate and it was too hot to quarrel. We both turned our attention to Monty, who had stood up and was patting the ball. Over and over again he danced and patted, using his nose to change direction. He practised all afternoon until he finally got control of the bouncy toy. Lesson one. Take charge of all situations.

Over the next weeks, we watched this odd relationship grow. Together they walked side by side in the olive paddock and when Jake slept in his chair, Monty lay beside him. When Monty got the 'zoomies' Jake would sit up and watch, checking, I believe, that the growing lad had developed perfect co-ordination over his body.

His student was maturing in leaps and bounds and I often wondered whether Jake offered his paw out, with an olive stone in it, saying the words, "When you can take the stone from my paw, it's time for you to leave, Grasshopper."

His final lesson on how to survive and become

King of the Valley happened with the arrival of Joan.

Antonio was supplying milk for our little ones. He was happy to do this but it was a lot of milk to give away. Rafael came up with a solution. Like many times before, as we were returning from the town, we met the small, jolly, but sometimes tricky ex-goatherder on our track. He wound down his window.

"I have left a gift for you English," he said while revving his engine, indicating that he was in a hurry to leave.

"Oh, how nice of you," I said. "What sort of gift?"

"A gift that will solve your problems with milk," he replied. "Now I must leave, my dinner will be ready."

And with that he disappeared in a cloud of dust while we disappeared into our thoughts. It was Pete who broke the silence.

"I dread to think what the hell he's left this time."

"Me too," I said, as I climbed out of the car and opened our gates.

Monty was barking madly inside the house while Jake slept soundly in the fruit bowl. The big gangly pup dashed past us and began barking at the goat shed.

"Oh no, I bet he's left another sick kid for us to take care of," I said.

"Don't be stupid, Diane. Rafael said he'd solved the milk problem."

We stood by the goat shed door, took deep breaths and walked inside. Alice, Pepita and Chinni were hiding underneath the feed trough. Carmen the lamb and Ruby were huddled in a corner. The reason for their terror was a large brown goat, standing in the middle of the shed. I stepped towards her and she lowered her head to charge.

"Go and fetch the collar and lead from my rucksack, Pete. She's either frightened or crazy."

Peter ran to the house, grabbed my rucksack and brought it back to the goat shed.

"You can find the collar and lead. I'm not putting my hand into that black hole!" he said, handing me the overloaded backpack.

I found the lead on the first delve, which was a bloody miracle. I began to approach the goat, speaking in a silly voice in the hope that it would relax her.

It didn't.

"Plan B, Pete. Food."

Pete again dashed to the feed room, grabbed a bucket and threw a handful of goat mix in before jogging back to the goat shed and leaning on the door to catch his breath.

"You rattle the bucket and I'll sling the lead around her neck," I instructed, with more confidence than I felt.

The little ones hadn't moved from their hiding place. Only Ruby showed interest in the rattling bucket but as she moved forward, the brown demon lunged at her.

"Rattle, Pete, rattle louder!"

As Pete rattled, the brown demon raced forward, shoving her head into the bucket. I swiftly looped the lead around her neck.

"And now?" questioned Pete.

"Now we get her out of the shed. Start walking backwards."

Without missing a beat, we both broke into a chorus of *I'm walking backwards for Christmas* by The Goons as we slowly waddled our way to the door. Unfortunately, as we opened it, I realised that there was a flaw in the plan. Peter hadn't factored in the brown demon's eating capacity.

By the time we'd passed through the portal and closed it, she'd scoffed the entire contents of the bucket. She took off like a cannonball into the paddock with me hanging on to the lead for dear life. Suddenly, *The Goon Show* had turned into *The Benny Hill Show*, with Peter's hysterical laughter overpowering my frantic screams.

"Phone Rafael!" I shouted over my shoulder, after my third lap around the paddock.

By the time Pete had made the call, the goat had stopped dragging me around the field and had begun munching grass. I quickly pulled a collar out of my back pocket and fastened it tight.

"What did Rafael say?"

"Well, apparently her name is Juana and she was a pet to a friend of his," said Peter. "He told me that she hasn't mixed very well with other goats but has lots of milk. Then he put the phone down."

"Oh, bloody great!" I snarled. "Loosely translated, she has been a weed clearer, become unmanageable and dumped on us."

"Terrific. So now what?"

"Plan C. Phone Antonio!"

Antonio didn't understand Pete's garbled message, but a few moments later, like the genie of the lamp, appeared at our gate.

"What have we got here?" he asked, reaching for his tobacco.

"A crazy goat sent to us with love from Rafael," I replied.

Antonio walked around Juana/Joan and took a long look at her teats before taking the lead rope from me and walking her back to the goat shed. At the sight of Antonio, our babies crept out from underneath the feed trough. Carmen, however, remained in the corner to watch how events would unfold.

"Diane, get Alice and I'll get her to latch on. Pedro, hold on to Juana and don't scare her," El Maestro instructed.

"Don't effing scare her!" muttered Pete under his breath, as he grabbed the lead from me.

Alice squirmed out of my arms and launched herself at Joan's teats, not needing Antonio's help to connect with the milk bar. In a nano-second, Joan erupted, knocking Pete off his feet and running madly around the shed.

"What now, Antonio?" said I.

"The thumb," said he.

He grabbed the goat, pushed her up against the wall and turned to me.

"This won't hurt her and will give you total control, trust me."

He put his thumb into her mouth. My eyes widened.

"Ruby," Antonio called.

Our little blonde girl ran over and began to suckle. Joan didn't move. Result! After Ruby had finished both sides, Antonio manoeuvred Joan outside.

"Diane, put her in the tiny paddock behind the house. Phone Rafael and tell him to come and get her."

"But Antonio, can't she be tamed?" I said.

"No. In my opinion, no. Sorry, but she could hurt the kids. Get her gone as soon as possible."

I watched him leave, shaking his head.

Pete phoned Rafael and he promised to collect her at the weekend, but the weekend came and went. We phoned again and he promised it would be this coming Saturday. Monty hid when we brought Joan out from the paddock. Her pushing, shoving and head-butting everything in her way, unnerved him. Jake however, watched from his deck chair with, so it seemed to me, an amused look, tapping his paw on the side of his chair.

Joan was unmanageable, but one small slip from me changed everything.

I was in a hurry to feed Joan in her small paddock. I wanted to prepare dinner before the days chores took over. I didn't put the latch on the gate and Joan escaped.

We were alerted by the crashing of three outdoor chairs, and Monty running flat out into the house with his tail between his legs. Everything seemed to happen in slow motion. Pete and I ran out of the house but were brought to a halt as Joan spotted Jake and began making her way across the yard to head-butt him.

We didn't know whether to run, walk or just stand very still. We stood, almost mesmerised by what happened next. Monty bravely stood between us, observing the drama.

Jake slowly uncurled himself from his sleeping position and stepped down from his chair. Joan came to a halt, a foot away from the cat. Jake walked up to the brown demon and maybe, just maybe, he whispered that wonderful line from the movie, *The Outlaw Josey Wales*.

Jake

"Well, are you gonna pull those pistols, or whistle Dixie?"

As Joan lowered her head to charge, Jake hit her with a straight left and a right cross, before rattling her with a combination that rocked her back to the Stone Age. Joan collapsed in shock, while Jake just turned around and jumped back up onto his deck chair. Pete rugby-tackled the goat and between us, we dragged her back to the paddock.

Jake and Monty were left alone. What passed between them that day, we'll never know. Monty had learned a lesson that in his adult years he would be crowned as the King of the Valley. He learned calmness from Jake; to focus and never to back down, and that a fight is mostly won in the mind, with force being the last resort.

Rafael picked Joan up the following day. I confess I didn't ask where she was going next. I, or rather humans, had failed her.

Monty could now take the olive stone from Jake's paw and it was time for Jake to leave. And time to leave, it was.

Jake fell asleep on his deckchair a week later. But it was the deep sleep, the sleep that leads to the rainbow bridge.

2

Martin

My phone rings and reminds me I really must change the ringtone. The calypso alert is getting on my nerves. The trouble is, I'm not a seven-year-old child, so I'm not sure how to do it.

"I am in the Lost Garden," says Antonio.

The Lost Garden is a shaded area where we often rested when the day was at its hottest.

"That's nice. And..?"

"And, are you bringing your *cabritas* here today?"

"No, I'm going downriver," I say, now wondering what the real reason is for the phone call.

We haven't exactly fallen out but I am really fed up with arriving home in the dark. I'm also really fed up with continually pointing out that I have washing to sort out and a dinner to cook, as well as goats, horses and dogs to feed. He, of course, has electricity, hot water, food on the table and all his clothes washed and ironed for him. It had come to a head when I pointed out that "there is life after goats."

My friend, neighbour and goat expert is obsessive about animals. He cannot understand why I would not want to spend every moment of daylight out with the goats and so my words cut deep. He had sniffed and walked off. I was beginning to enjoy the extra half an hour in the town, meeting friends for coffee and a catch-up before taking to the hills with the goats and getting home before dark. It allowed me time to hang washing on the line, prepare food and just enjoy being at home, watching the setting sun with Pete and a glass of wine. Antonio must be getting bored, not having me to boss around.

"I have peanuts for Alice," he says. "I'll see you in twenty minutes."

I stare at my phone for a few seconds before shouting to Pete.

"Antonio has ordered me to meet him at the Lost Garden."

"Good luck with that," he says. "I've got to fix the fence that your fat horse has trashed – again!"

I want to defend my big old boy, but in truth

he does trample fences every other day, putting holes in them with his huge hooves. The goats take full advantage by escaping through the holes into our neighbour's olive groves. I escape quickly to get out of ear-shot as the air around our falling-down house will be turning blue when Peter can't find his wire cutters.

I whistle to Monty and my little water dog, Paz. Paz is now in semi-retirement as her arthritis is really giving her trouble. But some afternoons she demands to come with me and her dear friend. Monty and I lead the way up the narrow path towards Antonio's goat sheds. I can hear Paz rounding up the girls, using her little cockney voice to full effect.

"Get a bleedin' move on you rotten lot, and keep in line!"

We reach the sheds, and my plan is to take the shortcut, threading our way down through olive groves to the Lost Garden. The goats, naturally, have other ideas. They can smell the other herd and make a dash across the cliff of the opposite hill.

Paz shouts to me, "Don't worry, Mum, I'll take care of 'em, you take the easy way down. You're gettin' on a bit."

"Monty, are you staying with me?" I ask my bodyguard. "Paz seems to have everything under control."

"Well, one must take the easy path in life if one is offered it," he replies in his Prince Charles voice.

We finally round the last bend to the Lost Garden and I can see my girls mingling with Antonio's herd. Alice, I observe, has already made a beeline for her friend, who is sitting on a log by the river. By the time I reach Antonio, Alice has devoured a whole packet of peanuts.

"Hello, stranger," he says. "Have a cake."

He hands me a little pastry thing which, I assume, is a peace offering.

"Thank you," I say, stuffing the cake into my mouth. I show Alice my hands and say, "All gone!"

Alice turns swiftly back to Antonio, shaking her horns. He is ready with an orange.

"Eat Alicia, eat!" he says smiling, then turns to me. "I have sciatica."

"You have sciatica? No, no, no!"

My friend, who is around five feet and six inches in boots, has a back that is as strong as an ox. In all the years of working with him, he has never complained of any backaches. Unlike his English friends who complain every other day.

"I can sit to milk, but getting up is difficult," he says, rubbing his back.

"Right, Antonio, Pete will come up and help you carry the milk churns to the Land Rover tomorrow."

"It's alright, I can manage. I want you to see young Luca," he says, standing up carefully.

I follow him as he hobbles into the middle of the long field that we call The Lost Garden. Both herds have started to climb the hill, heading away from this good grazing.

"Watch this, Diane," Antonio says, and begins to whistle.

The young dog, Luca, springs into action and with the help of his mother, Chivvi, he works the herd back towards Antonio.

"Wow, he's very good, maybe another Julio?" I say, referring to a dog he had before we moved to Spain. Julio is always mentioned with the greatest reverence.

"It's too early to tell. He may get close, but needs more time," he says, placing both hands on his back.

"Shall we walk?" I ask. "It may ease your back pain."

"Good idea. Let's walk and watch Luca's every move, and see how good he might be."

Antonio's training skills were legendary amongst the *campo* workers and he was forever having dogs left at his sheds for him to train.

"It's not the dogs that need training, it's the owners," he would tell me.

He finally put a stop to it when he trained a dog named Rocky but when the owner came to pick him up, the man got angry when Antonio said he needed to come and work him for a week under his supervision. He didn't hear any more of Rocky or his fate. It upset him and he said he would never again take on another dog to train.

Then Rafael left a sack inside his shed whilst Antonio was walking the goats. Rafael phoned him.

"Antonio, I have left you a gift," he said.

Next, my phone rang at 8 pm.

"I need antibiotics, have you got the new bottle of Amoxicilina? Oh, and Rafael has done it again."

"Okay, Antonio, I have the antibiotics. I'll be up in fifteen minutes."

Peter was taking some time out to play guitar, thus having a good excuse not to accompany me to Antonio's sheds to see what Rafael had left this time.

It was all quiet in the sheds. The dogs were asleep in the top paddock and didn't even bother to bark when I arrived. I opened the big door and found Antonio sitting on a beer crate, talking to a goat that was tied up by the feed trough.

"I have the medicine," I said. "So, what has Rafael done now?"

He rose from his crate and took the medicine bottle from me before pointing to a large sack, lying on the floor.

"What's in it?" I asked.

"Apparently, a puppy," he said, drawing the medicine into a syringe. "Don't open the sack, it's going straight back tonight. No more dogs!"

I, of course, ignored him and opened the sack.

"It's empty, Antonio."

"Shit, it's escaped! Find it and put it back inside the sack."

His stern attitude surprised me, but I understood. If he held a puppy he would melt and not be able to hand it back.

"I've found it," I said, as I spied a small brown blob under a feed trough.

I picked up the tiny little brown pup and held it tight to my chest.

"Are its eyes open?" asked Antonio.

I examined the little thing.

"Barely," I replied. "And it's a boy."

Antonio magically appeared at my shoulder.

"Give, give, give," he said, sounding like my goat, Alice.

He examined the little mite, cuddled it and started making odd sounds, which I took to be Spanish 'cooing'.

"He's a sweet little thing isn't he, Antonio?"

"He should be with his mother!" he said, spitting the words out as he held the pup high in the air. "I name you Martin."

I blinked a few times before Antonio dropped his bombshell.

"He can't stay here. He is too young and I wouldn't trust my dogs with him," he said, handing me the pup. "You have to look after him and be his mother for a while."

My blinking got out of control.

"What! *Hombre*, I can't have another dog! I have Monty and Paz and besides, Pete will go ballistic!"

"So, you want me to hand Martin back to Rafael? God knows what will happen to him," he said, making a pathetic attempt to remove Martin from my arms. He knew I would relent.

"Okay, okay!" I said, closing my jacket around Martin and without another word, I made off down the track to face my dogs and my husband.

I stood outside the front door and listened, for a brief second, to Pete playing and singing *Stuck in the Middle with You* by Stealers Wheel.

"Appropriate," I muttered under my breath before entering.

"*Clowns to the left of me, jokers to the right, here I am, stuck in the middle with you,*" sang Pete, with a big smile on his face.

I couldn't clap, as my hand was supporting the pup under my jacket. Monty raised his head and sniffed the air as Paz walked over and sat in front of me. Her big brown eyes smiled.

"What you hiding, Mum?" she asked in her little cockney voice.

"What have you got in your jacket, Diane?" Pete asked, putting his guitar down.

"Ah, well, erm, I have a Martin," I said.

"A what?" said Pete, his eyes starting to narrow.

I walked over, unzipping the jacket and showing him the pup. It was a tiny Spanish water dog.

Paz was now joined by Monty, and I began to gabble.

"You see, Rafael dumped him and Antonio's dogs will murder him, so I'm looking after him for a bit and I have to give him a feed." I finished by shoving Martin into Pete's arms.

I looked to Paz for backup. She sniffed the pup's bottom.

"You can't take it out on the kids, Dad," she pronounced, and Monty seemed to agree with her.

"Well, of course not," Monty answered his friend, in his Prince Charles voice. "One must give shelter to those in need."

At least, I think that's what he said, as they

both seemed mesmerised by the little mite. Pete found his voice.

"What sort of name is 'Martin' for a dog?" he said, stroking the pup's head.

"It sounds better in Spanish. Marrrteen," I replied, fishing out a jug of goat's milk from the fridge to warm up.

"I'm going to put him on the floor to see what Monty and Paz think," said Pete, placing Martin on the floor by Paz. The pup began to waddle, and Paz helped him towards the front door with her nose.

"See, Diane, Paz wants him gone," said Pete.

Paz looked at me.

"Open the door, Mum," the look said.

Paz has the ability to tell me what to do very clearly. I opened the door and Paz pushed Martin outside. Martin immediately had a wee. Paz waited until he had finished and then, using her nose, pushed him back inside. She paused to look at me.

"When you 'ave to go, you 'ave to go," her eyes told me.

I put some warm milk into a dish and prayed he would know how to lap. Paz assisted by lapping first, before standing back. Martin quickly got the hang of drinking and licked the platter clean.

"And now?" asked Pete, his eyes slightly softening.

"Ah, yes. Well, it's alright because, you see, I do have a plan," I said confidently. "I'll wrap him in a small blanket and take him to bed with us."

Pete reached for the brandy bottle.

And so Martin came to live at Las Vicarias.

The first week, he slept with us. He was no problem at all, as all I had to say to him was, "Nite-nite, Martin," and he would go to sleep. When I awoke, I whispered, "Morning, Martin," and that was when the day became a tad crazy.

As soon as his eyes opened and he was placed on the floor, he turned into a Duracell Bunny, on steroids. He had a manic energy that had to be seen to be believed. Like Paz and Monty, he didn't destroy, or chew, anything. Martin just 'whizzed'.

When Martin was three months old, Antonio thought we should walk him with the goats as soon as possible.

"We will know within a couple of weeks if he has it in him to be a good goat dog," he said.

After three weeks of walking with the herds, Martin failed his test. He tried hard to copy Paz but a bright stone would distract him, and the job in hand would be forgotten. He barked at, attacked and mauled the local geology. His escalating barking frightened the goats, and nothing either I or Antonio tried could re-engage Martin's brain.

Antonio will not give up on a young dog

quickly. He has great patience and looks for ears, eyes and small muscle movements that show the pup is trying to learn. Sadly, Martin gave him nothing to work with, and for the first time, Antonio admitted defeat.

Martin

"Diane, it's no good," he said. "Martin has given me no sign of ability. I'm sorry, but he can't come out with the goats anymore, he is upsetting them."

I knew he was right, but now what? Martin came home, and after all the dogs had eaten their dinner I told him to go to sleep, which he did, snuggling up to Monty. I needed to talk to Pete without interruptions.

"Martin won't make a goat dog, he has to stay

at home," I said, closing my eyes and bracing myself for a lecture.

"That's okay. He can stay with me and keep me company," he said.

I tried not to cry, but a tear did slip down my cheek. You see, every animal has a job to do, no matter how small. We all have to earn our keep, but Martin had become the exception.

How wrong we were. Martin would prove his worth and earn his keep, in a way we could never have imagined.

3

Katy

I arrive at Antonio's sheds and find Antonio, eyes closed, and resting on the side of a feed trough.

"I'm here, Antonio," I call out. "Let's move the milk churns to the Land Rover."

He straightens up and a wide grin greets me.

"My back is a lot better today."

"Oh, Antonio, that is fantastic news."

"Oh yes," he says, still smiling. "It's a lot better. Only my stomach hurts now."

"WHAT!"

"Stomach, it's playing up. Chari insists I go to the doctor," he says, rolling a cigarette. "I can't see the point, it will pass."

The phone interrupts his rolling. Chari, his wife, is calling.

"That early?" he says, into the phone. "Oh yes, okay. I'll be there."

"Doctor?" I ask.

"*Si*, appointment at 5 o'clock today," he says. "I have babies to sort out. This is ridiculous, it's just a tummy ache!"

"Antonio, how long has it been hurting?"

"About three weeks," he replies, with a shrug.

Antonio is stoic, he really doesn't complain about anything. No, wait, that's a lie. He did complain about the indignity of having a tetanus jab in his butt after slicing his knee open with a small axe. At the time he was up a tree, cutting down branches for the goats to eat. He knew it was a serious injury but decided to carry on his afternoon herding the goats, and wrapped his white vest around his knee. Five hours later, when he arrived home, his wife immediately drove him to Accident and Emergency.

To this day he claims that Chari was more upset about the bloodied vest than his wound. I am not sure that is true. She was probably angry that he didn't phone her and didn't head the goats back home straight away. Now I am angry that he hasn't told me that he has been in pain for weeks.

"Diarrhoea? Constipation? Sharp pains?" I ask, rattling out possible symptoms.

"No, just a dull ache," he says, as his eyes close for a second too long.

"The milk can stay here in the cool. I'm taking the goats out now," he says, picking up his walking stick and whistling to the dogs. "I have babies to sort out later, so best be off."

I walk slowly back down the track to the farm, puzzled and quite concerned.

Antonio's dedication to ensuring all the kids have had enough milk and have been checked over thoroughly, means his days are long. With only him to look after around 150 babies, he often does not exit the sheds until 11 pm. Pete and I are exhausted from taking care of around sixty kids. Antonio's speciality is encouraging reluctant or weak kids to latch on to mum's teats.

"Patience, Diane, all you need is patience. Patience, good knees and a strong back."

There are different techniques I use to get a baby to latch on. Squirt a little milk onto its nose to open its mouth. Slip in a teat and clamp its mouth over the teat. Then wiggle its head. All quite easy if Mum stands still. But if she starts to hop away, her back leg needs to be firmly held. To recap. Kneel under goat, grab goat's back leg, shove baby up to Mum's teat, swivel wrist and squirt teat onto baby's nose and pray.

Technique number two. I scream for Pete.

"Hold her back leg before she tramples me to death!"

When my husband obliges, I can open the mouth and insert the teat. Then the wiggling begins. Whoever is dealing with the kid needs hauling to their feet, as knees and back are screaming for mercy. Antonio manages all this on his own. Mind you, he can roll a cigarette with one hand so that must give him an edge.

One morning, I popped up to retrieve the bottle of multivitamins he had borrowed three days before. I found a little black and white speckled baby underneath a feed trough, with no mother in sight.

"Hello, little thing," I cooed, realising then that this was a sick baby.

"ANTONIO!" I shouted, "WHERE ARE YOU?"

"Up here," came a voice from the back of the sheds. "I have three little ones to sort out."

Stumbling over dogs, goats and loose kids, I found him kneeling down, chatting to a goat and her babies.

"Now look," he said, addressing a little brown kid, "here is the milk store. Open mouth and drink."

I knelt down and watched as the baby opened its mouth and suckled.

"How do you do that and make it look so bloody easy?"

"Years of practice," he said, grinning.

"What's wrong with the baby under the feed trough?"

"Ahh, she won't make it. She can't suckle and is very weak."

"You can't get it to latch on!" I exclaimed, not believing Antonio would admit defeat.

"No, I can't. Something is wrong with her and I have to leave her until the last to feed. I am at my limit."

"Can I take her?" The words just popped out of my mouth.

"You can try but I don't think she will live." He turned back to put another baby onto a teat.

"Can I take her now?"

"Yes, yes, take her." He resumed chatting to the babies who were waiting their turn for milk.

I returned to the feed trough, tripping over his sleeping dogs en route. I bundled the little kid inside my coat and wondered how Pete and the dogs would react to this latest little problem.

When I reached home, Pete was not in the house. I could hear him sweeping outside and swearing; his back was playing up again. The dogs were asleep in front of the fire. Before talking to Pete, I placed the baby in a cardboard box and covered her with a blanket.

He took the news that there was a sick little kid lying in a box on the kitchen table quite well, I thought.

"And what, may I ask, has Antonio called this one?" There was just a touch of sarcasm in his voice.

"He hasn't. He doesn't think it will live long."

"That's never stopped him before."

"Perhaps we shouldn't name her until we are sure she has a fifty-fifty chance," I said. "Right. Let the girls out and then I will make a plan for 'Tiddles'."

My final plan was to get her to drink from a bottle five times a day. Little and often, to build up her strength. It didn't work. She developed a very bad lung infection. I gave her antibiotics plus bicarb of soda, then an enema to ensure that there was no blockage in her bowels.

"Diane, I have been thinking," Peter said one evening.

That statement should have been met with half a dozen quips, but I was too concerned about little Tiddles to reply.

"She could have a cleft palate," he continued.

"Pete, the milk does not come out of her nose when she drinks. She can't have one," I said, my mind now racing.

"Torch!" we said in unison.

Pete grabbed his and I prised her mouth open.

We peered in, took a sharp intake of breath and let her mouth close. Locking eyes we both said, "Shit."

The roof of her mouth was one large hole. I had never seen anything like this before.

"Well done, Pete, the mystery is solved."

"So, now what?" he asked.

"Now I go and seek help from the internet," I replied.

Paz and Monty followed me to the river, to find a good signal. My youngest daughter, Felicity, had sent over a posh phone but I kept getting the name wrong and called it my Strawberry. The name stuck. I pulled out my trusty Strawberry, and began to search for information.

Monty sat on my right and Paz on my left, like odd-shaped bookends, while I read and absorbed every bit of info on 'cleft palate in a goat'.

The conclusions were not great. The vet sites thought euthanasia was the only course of action. I began to rise from the flat rock I was sitting on. The two dogs didn't move.

"She is a hopeless case," I told them.

No movement from my canine friends. No words of comfort. No, "Come on, Mum, 'ave a nice cup of tea, that fixes everyfing," from Paz. No, "Mummy, one cannot save every little creature," from Monty. They just sat and stared off into the distance.

I sat back down again on my rock and thought some more. Goat farmers in America may help. I found a forum and put the question out.

Help, urgent, cleft palate kid, advice please.

And the advice came back.

This time, when I got up from my rock, both Monty and Paz wagged their tails and led the way back to the house.

"I have a plan, Pete," I announced. "Go and cut down some *alamo*, while we still have light."

Alamo is the name Antonio gives to a soft green-leafed tree. I have no idea of its correct name but that matters not. The goats love it.

"Okay, but what did you find out?" he asked, putting on his boots.

"The vet pages say she is buggered but the farm ladies say give it a go. They advised no milk, just tree leaves, bush cuttings, herbs and vitamins."

"Just as long as she eats the stuff," he muttered, as he walked away with his trusty saw.

We tied up the branches and hung them, 'kid height', in the kitchen.

"No more milk, young lady," I told her. "You have to eat this now." I pushed her towards the cuttings.

And eat she did. Slowly at first, but she kept at it.

"Now, we can name her," I said.

Katy

"Katy," said Peter. "I name her Katy."

Katy

We sat that evening, watching Katy steadily munching the succulent leaves. She had made it this far, but it wasn't us alone that had encouraged her to live. Martin had also. The little dog that was useless with goats had found his purpose in life. He was a carer.

From the moment Katy came to the farm Martin had cleaned her, slept with her, walked beside her to protect her from any danger. He sat by the fire next to her, watching the patterns in the flames.

Martin finally had a job. He was now part of 'Team Las Vicarias'.

Katy was the first of many kids he looked after. In time to come he took care of humans, too.

4

Blanquita and Bailey

"Answer your bloody phone!" my ever-patient husband screams.

"Oh, sorry. I can't get used to the ringtone."

Just working out how to transfer contacts onto my new phone is mind-boggling, let alone the minefield of ringtone options. Note to self: must ask Antonio's daughter, Rosa Maria, to sort it out.

"Hello Antonio, how are you?"

"Fine—come—cousin—information," comes the distorted, distant voice.

"Can't hear you, Antonio, where are you?"

"Cousin—olives—riverbed," he says, with a voice that seems to be speaking from underwater.

"On my way," I say. "Repeat, on my way."

The phone went dead.

"Is he okay?" asks Pete.

"I think so. The signal was so bad I could barely hear what he was saying. I'll take the girls out now and look for him."

I find Antonio sitting on a log under a eucalyptus tree by the river.

"How did the visit to the doctor go?" I ask.

"What? Oh, yes, the doctor," he says, rolling a cigarette.

"Well, what did he say?" I ask impatiently.

"Got to have a camera down my throat to have a look around," he replies, taking a large drag on his thinly-rolled cigarette.

"Oh, that's okay. They will freeze your throat and then a thin tube will go in and check your tummy."

I add a smile of reassurance.

"So, it won't hurt?"

"Don't be silly, of course it won't hurt. I know a lot of people who have had this done, and they said it was a bit uncomfortable, that's all."

"So… it won't hurt?" he asks again, squinting at me for double confirmation.

"No, it won't hurt. But why does your doctor want you to have this?"

"He thinks I may have an ulcer," he says.

Before I can reply, he whistles to the herd to move down the river bed to find fresh pickings.

"Okay. Apart from a suspected ulcer, how are you feeling in general?"

"I'm fine. Well, except for the smell in the kitchen," he replies.

This remark stalls me for a moment and my mind begins to whirl.

"What smell in the kitchen?"

"The smell, the smell," he answers, frustrated that I don't understand him.

"Is Chari cooking English food?" I thought this would amuse him.

"No, no, all food smells horrid. I don't know why. Perhaps it's connected to my stomach ache." He begins to laugh.

"It is a new symptom, Antonio. Tell the man when you have the tube thing done."

"Okay, but you, too, have a problem," he says.

"I have a problem?"

Antonio points to the ground.

"Your horses have ducked under the tape last night."

I follow his finger and yes, there are hoof prints. Damn! Hardy and old Bailey had gone walkabout.

"Put a 'jump' on the fence tonight," he instructs. "One big electric shock should stop them."

"You told me to never do that. You said my battery could be stolen in the night."

"It's Monday, Diane. No one will be around tonight; it will be fine."

I take a moment to phone Pete with instructions to take our prized solar fencer upriver, and to put a good charge on the tape.

"Antonio, let's put your smell problem to the test," I suggest.

I call over my lovely big black buck, Rigsby. He snuffles up to me and I give him the orange I keep in my pocket for emergencies. Bucks pong. We are used to it and as our boys walk out in the *campo*, their pong isn't as strong as a housed buck. But nonetheless, they exude a strong whiff.

"Smell him."

Antonio bends and sniffs my boy's face.

"Smells fine to me," he says, with a big grin.

The puzzle of Antonio's illness has taken a new twist.

Beau and Hardy, our two horses, came over to Spain with us and had adapted well to the Spanish climate. Beau, a beautiful black and white cob, enjoyed walking in the river at dusk, cooling his hooves after a long, hot day. He amused himself watching the frogs croaking their songs to attract females. I loved watching him splash along the river and then stand, ears pricked, listening to the little green creatures belting out an aria.

Hardy, a huge bay cob, would follow his friend, sampling new foods that grow on the river bank. Occasionally, the boys slipped under the electric fence to explore upriver. Thankfully, my whistle (or Beau's inner dinner gong) bring my English horses back home for their 'hard feed', thus ensuring they get all the supplements that prevent sand colic. It also ensures that at 8 am and 8 pm, the two cobs arrive safe and sound at the paddock gate and have not extended a midnight walkabout upriver and got themselves into trouble.

I wanted to put a full electric charge on the fence to prevent the boys from limbo-dancing underneath, but Antonio was worried that the fence and battery would be stolen at night. Being new English in the *campo* and having already had our tools stolen once while we were in the town, I did as Antonio instructed.

When the mood took him, Beau would duck underneath the tape and stroll along the river banks upriver to eat fresh pickings, with Hardy in hot pursuit. My big boy has no sense of direction. In all my years, I have never met a horse that couldn't instinctively get its rider home without guidance. Maybe Hardy was too busy enjoying the countryside to take note of landmarks.

Or maybe he takes after his human friend, who can get lost on her own land. A shining example of my stupidity was on a first-time visit to Cadiz.

"We must get a landmark so we will know where we left the car," I told Peter. "Oh look, over there is a ship. That can be our landmark."

Pete stared at me for a minute, perhaps wondering how he came to marry this half-wit.

"Diane, the clue is in the word. LANDmark," he said in clipped tones. "A ship moves."

"Oh, right," I said, hoping he wouldn't dwell all day on my slightly ridiculous suggestion. "So, what shall we use then?"

"That bloody great cathedral over there might be a good idea." Now his tone was very clipped.

It didn't spoil the day but the story was quoted many times to friends, over cheese and wine, with me having a rigid smile and enduring the ridicule that flowed at my expense.

One evening at the farm, I began to pace outside as 8 pm had come and gone, with no sign of the horses arriving for supper. Pete immediately put new batteries in our torches in preparation for our trek upriver to find them. As I gathered up the head collars, we heard the sound of galloping hoofs. The light was fading fast now, and my heart didn't know whether to thump with relief or bang double time in panic. Hardy arrived at the gate.

"Where is Beau?" I asked him.

Hardy's face provided the answer. The big lad hadn't a clue and was now going into full panic mode.

"It's okay, Hardy. We are going to look for him," I assured him. "Pete, Beau's not here, he may be stuck, hurt or worse. Have the vet on speed dial."

My brain was racing. Hardy always stayed so close to Beau. What could have happened? I hurried to the river bank with Hardy trotting alongside me. I called Beau's name and both Hardy and I stood still to listen for a reply.

Nothing.

It was now dark and Hardy and I were following the beam of my torch, showing the way along the river bank. Pete had crossed the river, and was sweeping his torch from side to side on his river bank.

"Beau!" I called. "Where are you?"

Hardy now had his head resting on top of mine and we swivelled from side to side, straining our ears for his reply. Nothing came back.

"Your turn, Hardy. Call him," I said, willing my horse to understand. He did, and gave one loud whinny. We both cocked our heads to listen.

"Here he is," Pete called out.

And there, crossing the river, came Beau.

None the worse for wear but looked slightly bewildered.

Hardy dashed ahead to meet his friend while I trotted behind focusing my torch on his body, running the beam over his legs, checking for injuries. There were none.

Later, after we fed and locked them in the small paddock for the night, we worked out, as best we could, what probably happened.

Beau had stuck to his usual path up and then back down the river. Hardy had daydreamed and was left behind. Realising his compass had disappeared he made a dash for home, hoping he had run in the right direction. He had overtaken a munching Beau and arrived at their paddock in a panic. Beau, meanwhile, had ambled slowly home waiting for Hardy to catch up.

By not answering Hardy's calls, Beau was teaching him not to wander off. A bit like a child lost in a shop. The mother watches but allows the child to panic. In future the child must not go walkabout in a supermarket but must hold on tight to the trolley. It worked on my two daughters and it worked on Hardy. Never again did he lose sight of his friend.

Blanquita and Bailey

Rafael, our soon-to-be-retired goat herder from downriver, had a problem. His problem now became ours. His beautiful white mare, Blanquita, had a foal and now it was time to wean him.

"My problem will be solved," he told us, on a visit late one evening, "if you could look after the mare for a few months here at your good farm."

We could hardly say no, as Rafael had given us three starter goats, Alice, Pepa and Chinni, plus Carmen and Loretta the sheep. He also gave me my mastin, Monty.

"Of course she can stay with us," I said, avoiding eye contact with Pete. "Only, she may not get on with my boys."

"Blanquita will be fine, and you can ride her too."

The lovely, tall white Spanish mare arrived the next day. Rafael rode her bareback to us, over the hills and along the bumpy track, before leaping off and issuing orders.

"Open the gate and let her in with your horses."

"Oh no, Rafael. We must put her in the small paddock first so they can get used to each other. It's all prepared with hay and water."

"No," he said firmly. "They meet now!"

With that, he opened the gate, yanked off her bridle and gave her a slap on her rump. Blanquita began to neigh and squeal. The boys, at first oblivious of her arrival and grazing by the river, answered back. A truck had also arrived, driven by one of Rafael's friends. The little Spaniard jumped in and with a wave of his hand, gave instructions to his driver to get out, pronto.

"Bloody typical," said Pete. "We could be landed with a huge vet bill if this meeting goes wrong."

I muttered swear words, aimed at Rafael, and then muttered a prayer to the gods, asking that this meeting of two English horses and one very anxious Spanish mare, would have a happy ending.

We watched anxiously. After initial snorts, twirls and bucks, all three settled down. I thanked the gods. This first greeting went really well, all three talking the international language of Equus.

It seemed to falter after tea time. Small talk was exhausted and up came the language barrier. My boys spoke perfect human English. Beau, with a Dublin accent and Hardy, mostly in a Bertie Wooster voice, with the overuse of the words 'tally-ho' 'pip-pip', and 'what-ho'. Faced with this elegant Spanish mare, whose accent must have been very strong, the two English Cobs were stumped.

After half an hour, Beau lost interest in her, but Hardy persevered, and Blanquita fell in love. He walked beside her, chatting away and inclining his head towards her. She was mesmerised by this foreign giant of a horse. Beau left them to it.

I would love to say that over the following weeks the three equines became firm friends, but that was not true. Beau, although showing no outward hostility towards the Spanish mare, begrudged her presence. She had interfered with the bachelor life he and Hardy had become accustomed to. The field shelter had become crowded, with Hardy standing in the middle of his two friends, keeping the peace as they sheltered from the fierce Spanish sun.

During the day, Beau would graze just slightly away from the two lovebirds. The sight of Blanquita licking Hardy's face and then rubbing his head with hers was just too much. It was passionate love on her part, but perhaps just "a jolly nice gal" on Hardy's. Early one Sunday morning, Blanquita was to prove her love to her English amour.

Our Spanish guest, Blanquita, did not display the same love towards us humans as she did Hardy. My attempt to groom her and generally fuss over her was met with flattened ears and a hind leg fully prepared to lash out. Tacking her up for a ride took courage and swiftness of foot to leap away from teeth and hooves, but once on her back, she was a dream.

She was so safe that I let my daughter take her

out alone in the Spanish *campo*. I had faith she would bring her home safe and sound. When she was turned back out into the paddock, Blanquita would rush to Hardy's side and smother him in kisses. Beau would sulk until his favourite human, Felicity, jumped on his back and rode him around the land, far away from the courting couple. Beau's handsome nose had been put out of joint, and on this early Sunday morning, when Hardy had a slight mishap, he declined to come to his friend's rescue, leaving the Spanish mare to solve the problem.

The problem was that Hardy had managed to get his great hoof stuck in a fence. This is a common occurrence, with Beau alerting me with a loud whinny. I would grab the wire cutters and extract his large, dinner plate-sized hoof from the now mangled wire.

I had climbed out of bed early this particular morning. I wanted to get ahead with the dusting the house needed before daughter Felicity arrived the following day. The dogs were still asleep, enjoying the cool of the early morning. Pete grunted and turned over, hoping to catch another twenty-minute kip before the chaos of the day rushed in.

I sat at our table dipping a hobnob into my tea, marvelling at the resilience of this noble biscuit, when a banging at the door disturbed the household. Paz and Monty woke, their eyes searching the room. Bang! There it was again and both dogs began to growl. I peered through the gaps in the door and spied a large white figure. Opening the window shutters, I saw a white horse.

"Oh shit!" I said loudly.

I pushed the dogs into the bedroom, then gently opened the front door. A large white face greeted me.

"How did you get here, and what has Hardy done now?"

Of course, she didn't understand a word I said but stared in the direction of the big field. I grabbed my glasses from the table and followed her gaze. Yes, there he was, standing very still in the field, ears pricked and looking back at me. I grabbed the wire cutters (and his white saviour) and approached the now-trashed paddock gate.

The paddock gate was Spanish style, an old bedstead tied to a post with wires and string. In order to get to the front door of our house, Blanquita had pushed the bedstead over, breaking the string and wire. Nothing was going to stand in her way to rescue her friend.

I wondered, as I cut Hardy's hoof out of the twisted wire fence, how he had communicated to the mare to 'fetch the old gal'. It's just one of the many mysteries Pete and I have decided not to question. We accept that there is always a way to

EL MAESTRO

talk with another species. Just relax and let the magic happen.

Meanwhile, Beau was nowhere in sight, only appearing when the rescue was complete and the breakfast bell rang out loud. One long whistle from me, a universal communication.

For over a year, the lovely Blanquita lived with us until Rafael dropped the bombshell that he wanted to sell her. We had no money, but the gods must have been listening, as our friends upriver, Andy and Julie, decided that they would buy her. Blanquita moved on to a 5-star residence, leaving Hardy and Beau to resume their bachelor life. Their friendship had weathered a third party and now peace, harmony and routine returned after the year of the 'mare'.

Always together, accepting each other's little foibles, until Beau left his friend for a journey that Hardy could not follow. All the precautions I took to prevent colic had failed. Beau left his human and his equine friend heartbroken.

A year passed and Hardy kept to the routine Beau had set, criss-crossing the river at set times of the day and arriving for morning and evening meals at 8 am and 8 pm. I looked for a companion for him, but none fitted Hardy's needs. Then our vet, Marina, found the perfect match. An old skinny Spanish boy who needed help.

My friend Eileen and I drove forty-five minutes away to see him. Yes, he was very thin and had an eye problem and a dry cough. My gut instinct, however, knew he was 'the one'. We made arrangements with Andy and Julie to pick up Bailey and transport him home.

Pete and I drove ahead with me giving him dodgy directions to find the *cortijo* that Bailey was living at. During the drive, I tried to prepare Pete for his initial viewing of Bailey.

"He's a bit thin and one eye is closed," I gabbled. "Oh, and he is very difficult to catch. But I'm sure Hardy will love him."

Pete grunted. Not fooled by my chatter, he had decided to make up his own mind up when he saw the horse. We all parked up outside the huge gates of the *cortijo* and waited for Bailey to be brought to us. The gate opened to a sharp intake of breath by the English.

"Bloody hell, Diane," said Julie.

"I hope he doesn't cark it before we get him home," said Andy.

I swivelled round to face Pete and waited for his opinion.

"He will be fine," he said, taking the lead rope from the Spanish chap. "He is very handsome."

Julie and Andy rolled their eyes, gently guiding Bailey into the trailer.

"He has great legs," said Julie, smiling at me. "Pete's right. He will be okay."

Andy just grinned.

Forty-five minutes later we were on our top track and unloading Bailey on the flat. Pete and I walked the old boy for the last fifteen minutes as the track dived downhill to the valley and became very bumpy.

"Good luck," our friends said, and drove away with cheerful waves.

I suspect they dissolved into hysterical laughter on their way home wondering how, yet again, their friends had been lumbered with a half-dead animal that needed tons of food that they couldn't afford.

The walk to the house showed us who Bailey was. He walked like a ballet dancer, his head held high, not spooked or pulling, just confident. This horse was once loved and respected. Bailey knew his worth. I later found out that all this was true. I also found out he had great speed. We put him in a paddock next to Hardy's big field shelter. I left Bailey to munch on grass and to get his bearings.

Hardy, who had been resting in the shelter, came out to see who this newcomer was. Pete sat next to me on an old garden chair placed by the paddock and passed me a glass of wine. We watched to see how both horses would react to each other. At best, there would be squeals and foot banging. At worst, kicking and lunging over the fence.

Beau, Blanquito and Hardy

There was nothing. Hardy stood still, ears pricked, staring at Bailey. The old boy looked up once then continued eating.

"This is going well," said Pete
"Yes it is, but it's flipping odd," I replied.
"Why odd?"

"Hardy's reaction should be different."

"Don't look for something to worry about," said Pete, getting up from the chair. "I'm off to play with Katy."

He left me pondering. What was my dear Hardy thinking? Was he asking himself, "Who is this horse? Is he a friend? What do I do?" Beau was not beside him to give instructions.

After an hour I saw Hardy move off to graze by the river to maintain the 'routine'. But I noted he didn't cross. He just wandered up and down the banks, keeping an eye on the paddock the newcomer was grazing in. Bailey had a feed and I left him to rest and take in his new surroundings.

After two weeks of eye drops, his eye was clear, his cough had ceased, and his lingering winter coat was now shedding. It was time to let him out to meet his new friend. Hardy was grazing just a few feet away from the paddock. I opened the gate and stood back, letting Bailey take his time to decide if he felt secure enough to leave the paddock, which had become his safe home for the past two weeks.

Somehow I knew it would be okay. Neither boy had raised their heads or squealed. Hardy waited until Bailey had walked out into the olive grove before walking slowly towards the river bank. Bailey followed. No more lonely nights for my big boy, and Bailey was now in a safe forever home.

Two senior gentlemen, free to walk in the beautiful valley of Las Vicarias.

5

Bridge crossing at midnight

"You lied," Antonio says angrily into his phone.

"What do you mean, I lied?" I ask, trying to hold my phone and pull a tick out of Patty's ear at the same time.

"You lied about the tube." His voice goes up another notch.

"I'm coming up to the sheds," I reply, ending the call.

Pete is in town and I am on tick duty. This is a nasty duty but I have become an expert at whipping out a tick from an animal's ear without leaving the head stuck in the skin. It's not a skill I boast about, but it is a skill nonetheless.

I gingerly step into Antonio's sheds, finding

him sitting on an upturned beer crate milking, by hand, the last in a long line of goats.

"What have I lied about?" I ask, continuing our phone conversation.

"The tube. The big black tube!"

Giving me time to absorb this information, he turns back to the tied goat and continues to milk. I buy more time by remarking on the 'cushions' he has made for the beer crates. He has stuffed two plastic sacks with foam and tied them onto the crates, providing extra bottom comfort whilst milking.

"Wow, what a great idea, Antonio." I hope that flattery will put him in a better mood.

"Why didn't you tell me the truth?" he says, his tone now that of a grumpy teenager. I carry the second newly-modelled crate over, and place it beside him.

"Antonio, please explain."

"The thin clear tube was not thin. It was the thickness of my little finger," he says, waving his digit in front of my nose. "And it was black!"

"Oh dear, so sorry."

"Oh, and they didn't numb my throat, they just shoved it in and told me to swallow," he says, closing his eyes at the memory.

"Of course, they sprayed your throat to numb it. Don't exaggerate." I couldn't believe my strong, hard, goat herder friend was being such a wimp.

"If they sprayed my throat it did not numb it, woman!" His voice has taken on a more indignant tone. "The tears rolled down my face. It was horrid."

A more sympathetic voice is needed.

"Oh Antonio, that must have been so uncomfortable. But what's more important is, what did the doctors say afterwards?"

"They didn't looked concerned, and we'll know more this week." He gets up to empty his full bucket of milk into the big milk churn.

"How do you feel, Antonio?"

"I feel fine," he says, twirling in front of me. "No backache, no stomach ache, I'm fine."

"What about the 'smell thing'? Is that still odd?"

"Not really. Chari seems to be bleaching everything and I hate that smell. But other than that, all is normal."

His mood seems to have lifted, and I move to the door to walk back down to the farm.

"I need some help when I get back from town," he calls out. "We have to redo the sandbags on the *vigas*."

"Okay. I'll bring my mattock and meet you there after lunch. Do you think the weather has settled? Any more storms to come?"

"Ahhh, Diane, you can never tell. The river has its own agenda.

The day began dank and grey. Birthing time was over and we had a lot of goats to hand-milk. It had rained for four days, nothing too dramatic, but enough to swell the river. Antonio and Pete had repaired the little makeshift bridge that we crossed to reach Antonio's hills. The recent rains hadn't inflicted too much damage. The plan that day was to take the goats high for a good long feast, as more rain wasn't due until late evening.

By 1 pm, both herds were gathered by the man-made bridge, ready to cross. I led the girls over and Antonio stayed by the bridge in case a goat got pushed off. Alice was first over, as she would topple any goat that got in her way. Carmen and Loretta, the sheep, were next. Chinni then led my girls over, followed by Antonio's herd.

We decided to take the girls by the old ruin first. A month earlier, Antonio's old girl, Sniffy, had taken shelter there when she got separated from the main herd in a storm. We would then slowly walk up his long green pasture, to the second big hill.

"Perhaps we will see the big white bull," Antonio said, full of enthusiasm. "He has been resting in my cousin's olive grove for two weeks now."

"Why?"

"Because he needs a rest, you know, after... well... you know."

He said this with a lot of head nodding, hoping I would understand.

"I don't know! And why hasn't his owner come to collect him?"

"Diane, he has been very busy with lady cows and the owner will come when he is needed again."

"Ah, I see. We would say in English he is 'shagged out'."

I am pretty sure Antonio hadn't a clue what 'shagged out' meant, but by the grin on his face, he'd got the gist.

"He just needs some peace and quiet, I think," Antonio said. "He is huge, so the owners won't be in a hurry to walk him home unless they have a cow to entice him."

I honed in on 'huge', my eyes now scanning the olive grove for a large, white bull. Antonio scanned the ground.

"He is close by," he said, pointing to fresh hoof prints.

I quickly pulled two lead ropes out of my rucksack and clipped Monty and Paz on. I did not want any heroics from my two dogs if we came across the bull. The goats walking ahead of us began to trot on the green pasture, before galloping towards the hill.

"I think we have found him," said Antonio, with a broad smile on his face.

"Antonio, look at my coat!" I said, pointing dramatically at the bright red post office jacket I was wearing.

Antonio shrugged his shoulders.

"Don't worry, I have a plan," he said.

"What bloody plan," I replied, keeping a tight hold on my two dogs.

"Watch," he said, and strode off towards the huge white bull that had now come into view.

"Keep behind me," he added. "And get ready to head towards the hill when I tell you.

It was at that moment the penny dropped.

I sometimes summon an alter ego, Clint Eastwood, to take over when I find myself in a tricky situation, Antonio calls upon Crocodile Dundee.

Paz, Monty and I watched as he extended his fist and lifted his little finger and forefinger. He started to hum while twisting his hand back and forth.

I quickly looked down at my two dogs, to see what they were making of this suicidal activity. Both were transfixed by the bull.

"I've got him, Diane. Move along and climb

up the hill to the goats," he said, then resumed the melodic hum.

I didn't look back. I began to run with the dogs and climbed up the hill, Monty dragging me up with the help of the lead. On reaching the herd I joined Antonio's dogs and goats, who were anxiously looking down at their human guide. We watched Antonio walk past the bull and the big white boy put his head down and continued eating grass.

"Always wanted to see if it would actually work as well as it did in the film," he said, striding past me on the narrow goat path.

He continued to hum all afternoon.

By late afternoon the clouds were getting darker, and I was getting a little uneasy.

"Are you sure the forecast was for rain during the night?" I asked him.

"That's what it said," Antonio replied, looking up at the sky.

We ziz-zagged along the middle part of the big hill. The girls could eat fresh herbs and keep out of the wind.

"Shit, Cassius Clay and Jackie Chan are fighting," said Antonio, pointing to the two *machos* butting heads on top of the hill.

It was then the first clap of thunder reverberated around the hills. We both turned to each other and said, "Shit!"

"Okay, Diane. Move the goats down quickly, and I will go up and get the boys."

I motioned to Paz to round the goats up, while Monty helped me negotiate the muddy paths. In order to get home safely before the storm kicked in, we needed to cross the bridge. It was about thirty minutes away. My head was bobbing up and down, first to the sky and then to the path. Carmen, the sheep, knowing we were in big trouble, joined me and Monty.

"Baaaaaaa," she called out to the goats in her operatic voice, which meant, "Move faster, you idiots!"

Paz had rejoined us after she, and her mother Chivvi, had pushed the girls further down the hill. I could feel Paz and Carmen were on high alert but Monty was being very calm and patient with me.

"Move along, Mummy," he said in his Prince Charles voice. "No tripping up. That's the ticket."

Antonio's voice came from behind me.

"Go! Go! Go!" he shouted.

I watched him run and jump, in a slalom ski fashion, down the hill, pausing to tell Chivvi to, "Move them."

Paz also went into action with my girls, rounding them up and pushing them hard down the hill. Monty and Carmen began to jog. I followed.

Bridge crossing at midnight

"Faster Diane! The river will cover the bridge in around ten minutes!"

I jogged, tripped and stumbled but kept up with Carmen and Monty. Antonio ran flat out towards the bridge, his green cape billowing out behind him. He had to get to the bridge first to ensure the goats crossed in single file. And to protect the three babies that had come out today on their first *campo* walk.

The rain came and the thunder crashed overhead. By the time I reached the bottom of the hill and was jogging on the path towards the bridge, God pulled the bath plug and it bucketed down. I finally caught up with the herds in the small old olive grove.

"Too late," said Antonio, breathing hard. "The river is over the bridge and it won't be long before it's washed to the side."

"Bugger!" I said in English.

Antonio collected wood and retrieved the dry grass and kindling that had been stashed inside a rock overhang, in case a *campo* fire was needed. Within ten minutes he had made a camp fire and goats, humans and dogs nudged toward the flames to get dry.

The rain had now stopped and Antonio went to the river to assess the situation.

"It won't be passable for at least three hours," he said, rolling a cigarette.

"Three hours stuck here! Oh God, I had better phone Pete," I said.

Of course there was no signal! I walked around the grove waving my phone in the air, hoping it would catch some intergalactic wave, but nothing.

It was now pitch black and cold. The stars popped out and started their twinkling dance. The goats settled to chew the cud while the dogs scratched out beds in the earth, snuggled down, and slept.

Meanwhile, back at the ranch, Pete had seen a flicker made by the campfire in the distance and worked out what had happened. He grabbed his torch, walking stick and rope before making his way to Antonio's sheds, then down the narrow, slippery path to the river.

The young kids were enjoying this adventure. They played for a while, and then snuggled up with their mums and drifted off to sleep. The two herds were happy to snooze together, a giant sleepover, fresh food all around and a warm fire. Goat bliss. Paz had one eye on me every time I got up to check the river. Monty was wide awake and had his great nose lifted in the air, sniffing for any potential danger that the night may bring.

Pete had arrived at the far side of the river and, in conversation with Antonio, tried to work out a plan. It seemed that the plan was to sit on either side of the river and talk football for half an hour.

I thought it best to sit next to the dogs and enjoy the stars, only occasionally distracted by farting goats. I felt myself nodding off to sleep. Then Antonio jumped up and startled all of us.

"I'm going in," he declared, and began unbuckling his jeans.

I was shocked.

"What are you doing?"

"I have to get in the river and fix the bridge, woman!"

I turned my back until I heard him slip into the river. When I turned around, I saw Antonio, holding his jeans and Wellington boots high above his head, walking towards Pete. He stepped onto the opposite bank and casually eased his boots back on.

There he stood in a black leather jacket, white underwear and welly boots. I got hysterics and Pete began coughing loudly, trying to hide my laughter. But Antonio heard.

"Diane, this is not the first time I have done this, nor will it be the last," he said.

He walked over to the bridge, which had swung sideways and jammed itself into the cane and bushes on my side of the river. My hysteria subsided to uncontrollable giggles.

"Pedro, bring me the rope," he said, ignoring me.

Peter handed over the rope. Antonio removed his boots and walked into the fast-flowing river. He tied the rope to the large logs, testing it over and over to make sure the knots were strong enough for what was to happen next. He walked back out of the river, threw the rope to Peter before putting his jeans and boots back on.

Antonio repairing the bridge

"Okay, Pedro, let's pull this bridge," he said. "Give it everything."

Bridge crossing at midnight

I stood up and so did the dogs. I think we all sent prayers up to help the two men heave the heavy bridge back into place. Pete was the anchor man, positioning himself where the bridge had to be placed, feeding the rope around his waist. Antonio dug into the sand and hauled the logs bit by bit across the river and along the side of the bank, with Peter taking up the slack and pulling with him.

"Close, Pedro," gasped Antonio. "We are nearly there."

I watched the handshake as the bridge was put back in place. It cleared the river, and it was time to cross. I called Monty, Paz, Carmen and Loretta who crossed over quickly, and without fuss. Next came Alice, followed by Chinni and the rest of my girls. They didn't hesitate, even though the river was rushing underneath and it was almost pitch black.

Antonio's goats were not impressed by the valour of the Las Vicarias' herd. They refused to move.

"Pedro, shine the torch onto the bridge," said Antonio. "I will have to throw them over."

He grabbed a goat, lifting her by her horns and rump onto the bridge. Then he swung her to the very end, which gave her no option but to jump onto the bank. Hornless goats were carried to the middle. Over and over again, he carried and manoeuvred forty to sixty kilos of goat across the bridge without incident.

Until a baby fell in.

Pete had seconds to react. The river was flowing very fast and the baby went under. Pete moved the torch beam off Antonio, who was standing mid-bridge with a goat in his arms, and shone it on the river. The kid's head popped up, and Peter hooked the baby's neck with the crook of his stick. In one swift movement, he lifted it out of the river and onto the sand next to me.

"Got it, Antonio," said Pete.

"Light, Pedro, light!" said Antonio.

I rushed and retrieved the baby, holding her tight to keep her warm. Pete put the beam back onto Antonio and he continued to carry goats across. Finally, the last one was thrown over and the baby was reunited with her mother.

Three goat herders made their way up the long, steep path to Antonio's sheds at midnight.

"Another day in the office," said I.

"*Si*, just another day in the office," said Antonio.

6

Pups

Music, loud music, is drifting down from Antonio's sheds, destroying our early morning peace. We are used to our neighbour's summer guests boogying on down until 4:30 am.

Antonio loathes the loud thump-thump racket that the Spanish radio stations put out. In fact, Antonio does not like music at all, with the exception, perhaps, of Bruce Springsteen, 'El Boss'. He only tolerates flamenco when the guitar alone plays. As soon as the singer joins in, telling a story of unrequited love, he reaches for the radio dial, shouting, "For God's sake, pull that man's tooth."

And so to hear modern pop cascading out of the goat sheds piques my curiosity. As I arrive at

Antonio's sheds, I can hear manly banter. Walking in, I see Agustin.

"Look who's here to help with the milking," says Antonio, beaming.

"Oh, I can see alright," I say, conjuring up a Clint Eastwood drawl.

The last time I had spoken to the young Agustin, it wasn't pretty. He had removed my electric fence posts from the river and hidden them in Antonio's sheds. Antonio had seen them and called me.

Acting on the information, I found the thief in the town and with the aid of Clint, I promised him pain and destruction if he ever touched anything of mine again.

Although Antonio showed support and loyalty to me, he also had a huge soft spot for Agustin. Antonio had become Agustin's surrogate father. As a young kid, he 'hopped' school to find his friend, the only grown-up who really talked to him. The young man did not respond well to rules and regulations. He found reading and writing difficult so he gave up and ran to the hills to be with Antonio.

Try as he might, Antonio could not encourage Agustin to stay in school. But he could teach him to be a goat herder and to understand the *campo*. More importantly, when Agustin reached sixteen, Antonio wanted to keep him away from drugs.

He succeeded in two of his aims but sadly, the call of a wild life was too strong. Agustin's visits to the goats and his friend dwindled to once a year. Why was the young 'oink' here now? I raise my eyebrow in a Roger Moore fashion.

"I thought he could give me a hand milking so I can get on with a few jobs later. And he can earn a bit of money on the side."

I swivel my head to stare at Agustin who, to show off, is hand milking at top speed. He gives me a huge smile. He is a handsome young man, well-versed in disarming young ladies with the 'beam'. I, being an old bird, am not impressed. I sniff and turn again to Antonio.

"How are you feeling?"

"Me, I'm fine. I must have caught a virus or something but I'm fine now."

"Good, I'll leave you to it. Things to do."

I wave my hand in a royal gesture and go. I have an uneasy feeling. I don't think Antonio is telling me the whole truth. Or maybe I am becoming a little paranoid. I need a relaxing goat walk.

No hills today, just a gentle wander downriver. I have no worries that the goats may dive into the newly-planted olive grove by the river banks. I am not concerned at all for I have Rita Mae and she will take care of everything.

EL MAESTRO

Antonio and I argue within five minutes of being together. We clash and both of us have been known to flounce off in the opposite direction. It's hard, I know, to imagine a tough, macho Spanish goatherder flouncing, but flounce he does.

A good example was when I suggested that maybe we should consider, just consider, raising two kids for our own consumption in the winter.

"It would be hard, Antonio. But if we eat meat in the winter, surely it's a good idea to eat organic meat, free range, well-cared-for meat?" It was a cold November morning. He was feeding a kid at the time.

"Diane, we don't eat our own babies," he said, clutching the little kid to his chest as if I was about to rip it out of his arms. He turned in a theatrical way and flounced to the back of the sheds, daring me to follow him.

Of course, he was right, and in truth, I could not eat one of our babies, but his reaction was not that of a manly goatherder. Rather, more like an actor making a dramatic theatrical exit, stage left. I received the same reaction when I told him I had saved enough money for Monty to have the 'snip'.

"You can't do that!" he said, his eyes widening in alarm.

"It's best for him, Antonio. Less risk of cancer and no unwanted pups." I braced myself for the argument.

"NO, I mean it Diane, NO!" He reached for his tobacco. "That dog is magnificent and you must keep his bloodline going. How could you think of castrating, CASTRATING, Monty? He will never forgive you, he won't be the same dog. You WILL NOT DO THIS."

Two weeks later Monty had the snip. The following month Martin underwent the same procedure. Both recovered well and we ate bread and cheese for many days to pay for it. I was relieved it was done knowing my boys would not contribute to the many unwanted puppies being born all over the place.

Antonio, it seemed, had forgiven me for this 'terrible thing' and did not mention it again. Until the day he announced that Luna (his mastin, and Monty's best beloved) was pregnant and Monty was the father.

"What? How? When?" I spluttered.

Antonio had moved to his summer sheds, named the Molino, or mill, and I hadn't seen him for nearly a month when he phoned me.

"The day Felicity arrived and I took your goats out. Monty came too, remember?"

I thought back and yes, Monty had gone with Antonio on the day we picked up Fliss from the airport. It was unusual for Monty to leave the farm without me. However, I hadn't given it much thought as I was too excited about my daughter's pending arrival.

"Are you sure Monty is the father?"

I was upset that Monty's operation had come too late, but I couldn't hide the tiny pleasure I felt that Monty's bloodline would live on.

"When is Luna due?"

"In a few weeks. Chivvi is expecting too. Pirri is the father of her pups. Don't worry, I have good homes for the pups."

Two weeks later I visited the Molino to view Monty's offsprings. Two beautiful girls.

"This one is mine," he told me. "And this one is for Diego. He really wanted one of Monty's pups."

Antonio, in a rare empathetic mood, realised I was now experiencing inner turmoil. These girls were my Monty's daughters and I should have a say in their future.

"Diego will look after her very well," he said, holding up the lighter-coloured pup. "She will have a huge garden to run in and good food. Plus living in the *campo*."

I still couldn't utter a word but held the beautiful girl Antonio had chosen for himself tightly to my chest.

"You can name her," he said.

My eyes opened wide. This was a huge gift from the man who takes charge of naming everything.

When Pete and I first arrived in Las Vicarias, Antonio had a huge mastin named Puma. Sadly, he died a year later, and Antonio was devastated.

"In honour of Puma, I will name her Cheeta," I announced, holding the pup in the air and copying Antonio's naming tradition. "What shall we name the other one?"

We both turned to the pup lying on the straw bed next to her mother. A shaft of light came down from the cracked roof tiles onto the sleeping girl.

"Her name will be Luz (Light)," he said. "Chivvi is due any day now. I think she will only have two as she is not very big. And the good news is that Diego wants one of hers too, so everything will be good."

The summer heat was punishing. I stayed downriver, walking the girls on the river banks, using the thick cane for shade. I avoided the long trek to visit Antonio. I gave the excuse that it was too hot to walk the girls to see him, but in truth I wanted to keep my distance from Monty's pups. I didn't want to get attached, for the girls were not mine. Antonio had to bond with Cheeta and Luz's future was with Diego, a fruit farmer. That all changed with a phone call.

"It's Luz, she has had an accident," said Antonio, calling early in the morning. He sounded beside himself.

"Okay, okay, we will drive to you as soon as we have sorted the goats."

Pete drove along the main road to Olvera, then took the turn off to Antonio's father's *nave*, or agricultural building. We parked up and phoned Antonio to come and pick us up in his Land Rover.

Without a word, we jumped into the Land Rover and began the back-wrenching drive down to the Molino. Halfway down the pot-holed track, I couldn't stand the silence any longer.

"What's happened, Antonio?"

"It's my fault," he said. "I should have put the twine in the cupboard but I didn't. And Luz nearly strangled herself."

"What's happened?" asked Peter, who hadn't heard over the noise of the Land Rover's engine. Nor could he translate Antonio's fast explanation.

"Not sure," I said, "but it seems Luz has had a serious accident."

Antonio abruptly stood on the brakes, ricocheting both of us forward into the dashboard.

"We are about to find out," I said. "Brace yourself."

We followed Antonio into the Molino and into the back feed room. There was little Luz, covered in purple spray and residual white surgical powder.

"What the…" I trailed off.

"She got entangled in bailing twine. It was my fault. I didn't keep it out of the way."

I knelt down to examine the little pup, which wasn't easy as her sister jumped all over me, wanting attention.

"So what's the damage, Antonio?"

"I took her to Bruno the vet," said Antonio quietly. "He wasn't pleased to have his Sunday disturbed but he looked at her, cleaned her wounds and said her front leg is now useless."

He then told me the story. Luz had played with the twine during the night and got tangled in it. As she struggled, the twine had tightened around her neck and leg. The wounds were quite deep but not life-threatening. I sat down on the straw to examine and comfort the little pup. It was then that the argument began.

"The vet just can't give up on her," I said. "There must be something he can do for her leg, she is young."

"He said the damage has been done and that's it!" replied Antonio.

Pete slipped away, leaving the two hotheads to argue the fate of the pup, and decided to examine Chivvi's little puppies.

"You have to take care of her, Diane," said Antonio.

"Why can't Diego take care of her? He wanted her after all."

"For God's sake woman, he won't take a damaged mastin."

This back and forth went on for some time until I realised that Antonio had made up his mind that Luz was my problem and arguing was a waste of energy. I now had to tell Pete.

I lifted Luz, wrapped her in a towel that Antonio had given me, and walked into the other feed room. Peter was playing with a brown puppy that I recognised as the pup I had rescued a few weeks earlier from a cliff when the little thing went walkabout.

It was quite a spectacular rescue. The stones I had used to climb the cliff gave way on our descent. Both pup and middle-aged idiot survived the fall with only a few of my goats to witness the event. No applause from them. Just a few loud farts as they walked away, giggling.

Pete was 'snoofling' the little pup with his nose.

"She is going to be a good goat dog, Pedro,

Pups

with Chivvi as her mother and Pirri for a father," said Antonio, proudly.

"Err… Antonio, Pirri isn't the father," said Peter, with a huge smile. "This pup's dad is Martin."

For a moment Antonio looked stunned. He snatched the pup from Peter's arms and stared at it.

"Of course it's not Martin's," he said. "Martin's indeed! This girl is Pirri's."

"She is Martin's daughter, Antonio," I said, peering over his shoulder. "There is no mistaking that face."

It was a good time to leave. Peter raised his eyebrows when we jumped into the Land Rover, looking at the towel that enveloped the little injured pup, Luz.

"I'll explain later when we get back to our car," I said, not wanting Antonio to witness a domestic between his two English friends.

The atmosphere in our car on the journey back to the farm was tense. On a scale of one to ten it was a definite twelve.

"What could I do, Pete? The puppy needs house rest and attention."

"You say NO."

"She is Monty's daughter," I said, in a little voice.

"And that other pup is Martin's daughter. Are we to have her too?"

"Don't be silly, of course not," I answered, as the car stopped abruptly outside our gates.

"Let's sum up, shall we," said Peter turning to look at me, eyes flashing. "We have a mastin, a water dog, Martin, who is definitely on the spectrum, and a cleft palate goat who snots green muck all over the house. Now you add a disabled mastin pup to the chaos."

I couldn't argue with that. Then inspiration flashed in front of me.

"Okay, okay, but Monty and Paz sleep in House Two now that it's hot. And think, if we can't re-home her, she can guard the farm when Monty is out with me."

"Straw and clutching come to mind," Pete replied, getting out of the car.

And so, Luz came to live with us. We called her Lulu. Paz was initially horrified. Monty was proud.

"Well, my dear, she is of royal blood," he told Paz.

"She is another bloody mouth to feed, that's wot she is," said Paz, never one to mince her words.

Martin loved her and Katy had a playmate, or rather a handy handkerchief, as she insisted on wiping her green snotty nose over the pup. The upside of this was she stopped using my trousers or the fridge door as a tissue to remove the excess snot caused by her cleft palate. But it was hardly hygienic. Pete came up with a brilliant idea to help the young pup and us. He tied a piece of sheepskin to the arm of one of our chairs as a nose wipe.

"She won't use it," I said.

"Oh yes, she will," answered Pete, picking up little Katy and gently placing her nose on the soft material.

And use it, she did. So much so that we had to cut out two more pieces so they could be kept clean and fluffy for Katy's nose.

Lulu's wounds had to be cleaned and dressed twice a day, but were healing nicely. Her paw, on the other hand, was just flopping about, and she walked on her knuckle, causing abrasions. I knew she needed physio to help her walk on this paw.

As her wounds began to heal, her personality emerged. She was a Princess in every sense of the word. She claimed the largest dog bed and waved her poorly paw in the air demanding, attention and food with the confidence of a debutante, ordering her first gin and tonic. She hopped around the house and yard, bestowing a royal wave of her wonky paw to all who stared at her.

Never once did she consider herself disabled. She was royalty, her father being King of the valley, and entitlement oozed out of her paws. Everyone loved her, as she was a hoot and always happy.

Lulu as a pup

Two weeks later Antonio arrived back at his sheds. Pete and I thought we should visit, as there had been a long silence between the two men. Antonio didn't want to push his luck by asking Peter to help him move back to Las Vicarias. But after two weeks, Peter had simmered down, and an olive branch, in the form of a can of beer, seemed to be the way forward.

Entering the shed, we were not met with the

Pups

boyish grin Antonio uses in awkward situations. We were met with an accusing snarl.

"How did it happen?" he said, glaring at me.

"Hello, welcome back and what have I done now?" I said, glancing at Pete who was putting the can of beer back into his jacket pocket.

"When did you allow Martin to go with Chivvi?"

"So you admit Martin is the pup's dad," I said, beginning to laugh.

He grabbed the little pup, who was hiding under a feed trough. "I can't keep one of Martin's offspring, it will be useless."

Peter stepped forward, reached in his pocket and handed the can of beer to Antonio. I couldn't work out what was going on. He then took the brown curly-haired pup from Antonio and lifted her in the air.

"I name you Rita Mae," he said, then turned to Antonio. "Diane saved her and if you don't want her, she is coming home with us."

Antonio and I both looked shocked.

"No, no. I will find her a home. You have enough dogs, what with Luz and all," Antonio spluttered, not knowing if he should open his cold beer or wait a few minutes more to see how the conversation would go.

"This is the daughter of Martin, and we will

take care of her," said Pete, backing out of the sheds.

Antonio looked at me, eyes wide open and head shaking.

"Diane, she will be useless like her dad. You don't want to take her on."

"Martin is not useless, and I will train Rita Mae," I said, also backing out of the shed door.

I realised that Pete's love for Martin had overridden common sense. Antonio had used the word 'useless' and that had torn at Pete's heart.

"Enjoy your beer, I'll see you tomorrow," I said, waving goodbye.

I caught up with Peter, who was now marching down the track, pup snuggled under his jacket.

"What have you done? Are you mad?"

"I couldn't have him talk about Martin that way, and anyway you rescued her from the cliff, so it's a sign."

The only sign I could see flashing on our foreheads was 'mugs'.

And so Rita Mae joined the family. Paz shook her head and Monty sighed, then they both walked next door to House Two for some peace and quiet. Lulu wrinkled her nose and climbed onto Monty's bed, but Martin looked pleased. Katy saw a new playmate and 'boinged' around the table madly until she tripped over. Martin rushed to check she was okay and a calm came over the house. Rita waddled onto a spare dog cushion and curled up to sleep.

I had been full of bravado when I stated loudly to Antonio that I would train little Rita Mae. But I would give it a go, and hopefully, Paz would help.

Things didn't quite work out the way I planned. Both Pete and I had come to realise we had very little control over our lives. Sometimes you have to sit down, open a bottle of red and keep the faith.

7

Rita Mae

"*Hola* Diane, I need to speak to Pedro," calls a voice from the paddock, setting all the dogs into a barking frenzy.

"Pete, it's Agustin. He wants to talk to you."

My husband straightens his back from cleaning the feed troughs. "I can't understand a word that boy says. You had better come with me." He waves at Agustin.

Strolling to the paddock fence, I call, "What's up?"

"Have to sell some *chivos* (baby goats) at midday and I need your help counting the kilos."

"Why, what's wrong with Antonio?" Fear grows in my voice.

"Nothing. Except that he keeps falling asleep

and you know how fast you have to be dealing with those buyers."

I relay this to Pete, who can speak Spanish so much better than I do but gets lost with *campo* slang.

"Okay, no problem. I'll meet you up the track."

Agustin turns and jogs back to Antonio's sheds. I am confused and worried.

"Agustin is probably exaggerating," Pete says. "He's just finding an excuse for me to do the maths as he is rubbish at it."

"Perhaps I should come with you."

"No, I don't think so." He looks for an empty notepad. "Especially after your last explosion with the buyers and crying when a baby was weighed. Best you stay here."

He was right of course. I can't cope with the selling of babies. Antonio telling me, "The first ten years are the worst," hasn't helped a bit.

I am not cut out to be a farmer and neither is Pete. We hadn't thought goat farming through properly. We hadn't realised that the babies we had delivered, nursed and bottle fed would have to be sold, and how it would break our hearts.

I had a 'red mist' moment when someone manhandled a baby going onto the truck. Bruce Lee took over, and I kung fu-ed his leg, knocking him to the ground. I followed up by giving the group of men a lecture on animal welfare. It had a liberal dose of English expletives after every five Spanish words.

Two hours pass, and I wait for Pete's return at the farm gates. The dogs alert me that a car is on the track, and I open the gates. His face looks grim. As he turns the car to park, his eyes meet mine, and he shakes his head.

"What's happened?" I ask before he has time to turn off the engine.

"It's Antonio. He kept falling asleep. Agustin said he's been like this for a few days."

"I don't understand. Is he tired and just grabbing forty winks?"

"No, Diane, he literally falls asleep. He was slumped over the Land Rover's steering wheel, dead to the world, and only woke up when Agustin shouted that the lorry had arrived. He really wasn't with it at all."

I had to do something, but what? So many questions rush through my mind. His family surely must see the change in him, so what is being done? I need to talk to a member of his family. A plan is formulating.

"I'll phone Rosa Maria with the excuse that I need my ringtone changed. It's Saturday tomorrow, no school and so she will be free. Besides, she loves walking with her dad and practising her English with me."

"It's a plan, Diane," says Pete. "It's a plan."

Rita Mae was the perfect pup. Her father, Martin, escorted both her and Katy the goat outside to go to the loo in the yard. Lulu followed, waving her paw in the air, then claimed the old sun lounger for her day's rest. Paz would tip-toe into the main house for a quiet breakfast, leaving Monty to take over from Martin and entertain little Katy until her nap time.

Katy, like all our special needs animals, had become very independent, very bossy and had acquired a Lancashire accent.

"Cooom on, Montee, plaaaay, plaaaaay," she would ask the big mastin.

Monty, being the kind dog he is, duly played 'push the football with the nose', 'race and chase' and 'hide and seek' until Katy was exhausted.

"Time fur a nap, Montee. I'm fair knackered, me," she would tell him.

"Well, thank the Lord for that," Monty would say in his Prince Charles voice.

Lulu would demand her food be brought to her lounger. Martin and Rita would share a large bowl, taking it in turns to eat. Meanwhile, the two horses banged at the back gate for their breakfast. While I took their buckets to feed them, after adding grated carrots and apples, Pete started dishing out the goats' feed. By the time I found Pete in the shed, I felt I had already completed a day's work, and by the look on Peter's face, he felt the same.

"This routine has to change," said Peter, tying up Alice ready to milk her.

Alice, sensing Pete's mood, stood stock still and did not attempt to steal her neighbour's food.

"Diane, the animals have taken over. We have to take back our authority!"

"Agreed. Shall I make toast and tea?" I forced a big smile, and then we both heard the crash.

"Katy!" we said simultaneously.

I dashed back to the house. All the dogs were sitting on their beds, staring at the mess. Katy had tipped over a saucepan of milk. I could only stare at the little goat, who was, by now, jumping up and down in it. In fact, she danced around the kitchen thinking that this new game was a hoot. I looked at Paz.

"She's a bleedin' menace, Mum," she conveyed to me in her cockney voice. "That wot she spilt could 'ave been 'ot."

Paz was right. I lifted Katy outside, calling Martin to keep an eye on her, and began to mop. The dogs stayed on their beds, not attempting to help clean up the milk. This told me that they had watched and understood the danger Katy had put herself in with her bad behaviour. I needed to find a solution to the problem and I needed to find one very quickly.

After making a plateful of toast, I ventured back into the milking shed and told Pete of Katy's latest antic.

"Where is she now?"

"Outside playing with Martin, and I think Monty is helping too.

"Well, that's it. She is a danger to herself. She has to move into House Two. She can only come into the house when we are there to watch her."

"But Pete, she will be traumatised. She can't just be thrown out of her house."

"Oh, right. So you would rather she burnt herself then?"

He had a point. We needed a huge change in routine and Katy had pushed us into making it happen.

That evening, Katy was to sleep in House Two, where the hay and straw were stacked. Monty had taken to sleeping there, as it was cool in the summer and peaceful. Well, except for Graham, the snake, dropping in for a chat. Rita loved the comfort of the straw and being away from Paz's judgemental gaze. Katy would be safe and have company. I, of course, was a wreck.

"Think of her like a child having to sleep in her own room, Diane." Pete handed me a small glass of very cheap wine. "She has to learn sometime."

"She is disabled and probably frightened of the dark. She won't cope without Martin." I tried not to sob.

"For goodness sake, she has Monty and Rita. She is hardly alone and we have the outside solar light, which will light up the yard."

"Okay, okay. Let's put a bunch of *alamo* up for her to munch if she gets stressed."

"Already sorted. Now let's put her next door so she is settled before dark," said Pete.

Katy cried.

"I want to come in 'ouse," she seemed to cry. "I want Martin. I want me maaaam!"

Pete had to practically nail me to my chair, as I wanted to dash next door to cuddle her. Paz stared at me.

"It's called tuff luv, Mum," her eyes said.

"Yes, I know Paz, but she is so fragile."

Paz snuggled down on her cushion, muttering something like, "Fragile, my arse."

Martin had been told to go to sleep. He immediately sank into a deep slumber. Lulu examined her paw and flopped onto the other sun lounger we had managed to squeeze into the house to accommodate her needs. Fifteen minutes later, all was silent and we tiptoed to bed.

The following morning I put our new routine into action.

Katy did not seem at all traumatised by her new bedroom. In fact, when I popped my head inside the door, she was still fast asleep on a hay bale next to Monty. Only Rita pottered out to take a pee. I fed the horses their breakfast, mucked out the stable, took a deep breath and soldiered on.

The next bit of the new routine was walking the dogs, and Katy. Monty and Martin walked either side of the little goat. She took off.

"Oooo, look at me, I can fly!" she said as she leapt off a grassy knoll. Monty and Martin kept close to the dancing goat, which left me free to observe Lulu's walking progress. She was still using her 'wrist' to walk on. A surgeon friend had visited a few weeks earlier and suggested that, if she had her leg amputated, the risk of a bad infection would be eliminated. A dog could cope perfectly well on three legs. I really didn't know what to do to help her.

Meanwhile, Paz was trying to encourage Rita Mae to climb the river banks at top speed but with little success. After half an hour, I called the dogs to come together and walk back to the farm. Katy had found a bush to munch, and wouldn't move.

"No, I'm fine. Leave me be," she stubbornly answered me.

I tried, "We are leaving, Katy. Bye, bye." That

didn't work. It just worried Monty and Martin. The only course of action was to pick her up and carry her home, kicking and screaming.

With the dogs and Katy's breakfast doled out, I could finally enter the goat shed with mugs of tea.

"I think the walk routine is going to work," I said, handing Pete his mug. "They are all eating breakfast quietly but Katy is a bit of a problem. She loves picking out what she wants to eat in her own time."

"That's okay. I'll take her out with Martin later when I check the fencing, and she can have another visit to the 'supermarket'." He sipped his tea and wrinkled his nose. I am not the best tea maker.

For once, the morning milking and kid care went well, and we checked on Coco, our gentle girl, who was due to give birth in a month's time. Coco, in the past, has had multiple kids and this time was no different. She was huge, and because of this, we made sure she had extra food and vitamins. Lulu's paw needed more wound powder applied, and dressing. Just as I finished securing the vet wrap, my phone chirped into life. It was Antonio.

"I was watching Luz in your field this morning," he said.

"Yes. Well, I was going to talk to you about

her. I think we should consider amputation, to make her life easier," I said.

"WHAT! Cut her leg off? Are you crazy woman?" he shouted into his phone.

I held my phone away from my ear as the torrent of Spanish flew down the line, and I couldn't keep up.

"Speak slowly. I can't understand a word you are saying."

"Diane, Lulu's problem is all in her head," he said speaking in a clipped tone, trying to suppress his frustration with his idiot friend. "Look. Her brain needs to be distracted and then she will use her paw correctly."

"Are you sure? I mean Alec is a surgeon and he felt …"

"Diane," he interrupted. "Alec is a good man but he is wrong about this, trust me."

The following morning a miracle happened. The new routine of early dog walking before breakfast was underway, with Katy skipping to her new favourite bush. That left the dogs free to paddle in the river. Two mallard ducks were disturbed as they paddled alongside the river banks. Paz took off first, followed by Monty, Rita, Martin and Lulu.

Somehow, in the excitement of duck chasing, her brain did exactly what Antonio had said it would do. Lulu flipped her paw upwards to run.

When all the dogs admitted defeat, as the ducks took off and flew upriver, they walked back to find me and Katy. Lulu proudly walked with them, flipping her paw upwards and allowing her pad to finally touch the ground. I told Antonio, over the phone, the moment we got back to the farm.

"Lulu can walk. She can really walk on her pad!"

"Told you I was right," he said smugly.

I concede that the man was annoyingly right in his judgement of animals most of the time.

Until Rita Mae.

Rita Mae

Now Paz and Monty were getting a little older; I felt they should only work a four or five-day week. Monty needed a rest. Not only was he walking for up to eight hours a day in the summer, on returning home, he had to face Katy begging him to, "Play Monty, play!"

Paz had been working hard trying to train Rita Mae to be a 'hill dog' but had failed miserably. Despite having an abundance of patience for me and Monty, Paz found slow learners trying. It seemed to me that Rita just didn't have a great deal of confidence. Paz and I tried to encourage her, but she had no desire to leave me and run up a hill to deal with the goats.

I realised that Antonio was right. I didn't have the ability to train her to work with Paz. It was me, not Paz or Rita Mae, who had failed. I came to this conclusion after a day working close to home on the hill behind our house. Paz was exhausted, climbing up and down the hill, showing Rita how to work the goats. Paz kept one eye on the young dog and the other on Willow, Alice's daughter. Willow, however, took advantage when her teacher, Paz, was distracted and ran higher onto the prohibited hunting ground.

By the end of the day, my darling Paz was tired out. When the goats walked through a neighbour's olive grove near home, her enthusiasm to keep the goats in order had waned.

"I'm bleedin' well knackered, Mum," her eyes told me.

"Don't worry Paz, I'll keep them off the olives. You take a breath."

It was at that moment we both stared at Martin's daughter as she ran up and down the narrow track, keeping all the goats in a straight line. Paz and I looked at each other and then back at little Rita Mae. We had found her talent.

The following week, Paz and I took the goats downriver and put Rita to work. Paz stayed in front of the herd, keeping them at a steady pace. I was at the back, not allowing anyone to lag behind. This left Rita to put a stop to the girls entering the olive groves close to the river bank.

Not one goat passed her. She used no force, just her body language and speed, to keep the girls in a straight line and maintain order. Even Paz had to admit that Rita Mae was good. Our little girl had found her niche in the goat-herding world. All that was left was to impress Antonio. That opportunity came a few days later.

"We go to Valencia today, and we will need Paz to keep the goats in order. We have to guard both sides of the track as they have planted new olives," Antonio informed me by phone. I was extracting

Katy from her favourite bush. "Meet you at the *vigas* at 10:00 am sharp."

Katy kicked the blimmin' phone out of my hand, just as I pulled her from her favourite restaurant, and it landed on a sandy bank.

"Righto!" I shouted, hoping Antonio could still hear me.

Valencia is the name given for one of Antonio's grass fields, nestled between two large olive groves. It's a long trek to get there, hence the name. The tracks are lined with prize olives. We have to be on alert, and the dogs have to work hard.

As soon as Antonio saw me walking the goats along the river bank towards the *vigas*, he waved and moved off. It took me nearly an hour before I finally caught up with him. Then he saw Rita Mae.

"Where is Paz?" he asked, looking behind me.

"At home resting," I said, with a smile. I was met with a snarl.

"I told you to bring Paz. If any olives get wrecked you are paying," He turned away and continued to walk along the narrow pathway towards the main track to Valencia. An hour later we arrived at the track, lined both sides with young olive trees.

"You had better keep them off the olives, Diane," he growled.

While sending Chivvi (Rita's mother) onto the other side of the track, he and Pirri guarded the other.

Two hundred goats began walking on the track, and Rita and I got to work. Rita took Chivvi's side and I, Antonio's.

It was like watching a ballet dancer. Rita almost glided, back and forth along the olive tree line. Antonio was struggling to keep Pirri under control as he dived into the herd and scattered the goats, leaving Rita and Chivvi to get them back under control. When we finally reached the end of the track, goats, dogs, and goat herders ran to the well that held the golden water. The pure water that humans and animals drink as if it was heaven sent. Antonio bent down and stroked Rita, then turned to me.

"She did good," he said quietly, smiling at me.

"Yes, she did. She found what she is good at, Antonio. You told me that all animals have a purpose."

"Yes, I did, and I was wrong about her. She is half Chivvi and yes, half Martin. And it seems, that is a very good combination."

Rita and I beamed for the rest of the afternoon.

8

Medical Emergencies

Antonio's daughter, Rosa Maria, has agreed to come walking with her papa and me after I had phoned her the previous evening.

"I was coming anyway, Diane. I must practise my English, and I will change your phone's ringtone for you."

Apart from having my annoying ringtone changed (screaming, "Shut up! Shut up!" never tamed the monster) I want to find out if her father has been acting out of character and falling asleep at odd times.

I walk the girls over the river and meet up with Antonio's herd, which is grazing the lush grass on the river banks. Antonio is unpacking his lunch.

"A bit early for food, sir."

"Never too early to eat."

He opens a can of tuna.

Rosa Maria hugs me, then opens her hand to receive my phone.

"What tone do you want?"

"Something gentle please."

"Don't be stupid, Diane," Antonio chimes in. "You are deaf. Rosa Maria, put something loud, like a drum banging."

Rosa Maria smiles and winks at me. The goats graze and I begin to unpack my sandwiches.

"Plenty here," says Antonio, handing me bread and a large piece of *tortilla*.

Rosa Maria and I chat in English. To help build her confidence when speaking and not be embarrassed if she mispronounces words, I ask simple questions. My Spanish is appalling, and I blame Antonio for that. He is a terrible teacher. He rattles Spanish at machine gun speed and never corrects my answers.

"I understand what you are trying to say," is his stock answer when I question him about tense or the pronunciation of certain words.

Five minutes into lunch and I notice Antonio has his head on his knees and he is fast asleep.

"Papa has gone off again," Rosa Maria says quietly.

"Is he sleeping like this at home?"

"Yes, all the time. He must be very tired."

Medical Emergencies

Her voice quavers a tiny bit. It is time to take over.

"Antonio, Antonio," I say, touching his shoulder.

He slowly raises his head and we lock eyes.

"I just need a little sleep," he says, lying down on the sand.

"Rosa Maria, put my jacket under his head and I'll take the goats onto the hill. You stay here with your Papa."

Whistling the goats and dogs, I walk the herds across the river and onto Antonio's small hill. When the girls settle down to eat the lush herbs, I remove my phone from my pocket and dial his sister's number.

Birthing time is tricky. Pete and I, in our naivety, thought that watching our goats give birth to beautiful babies would be the height of our year, but it was not the reality. Don't get me wrong. When a healthy baby pops out, we celebrate. When things go wrong, and it's a matter of life and death, the reality of farming kicks in.

I had instructed Antonio to phone me if he had any difficult births, so I could learn. I knew that one day he wouldn't be available if one of my girls had a problem and I needed to be prepared for any eventuality.

The phone call came just as Pete and I took our first sip of the bed-time milky drink.

"Need some help? Bring sugar," he said and disconnected.

"Boots back on, Pete."

I grabbed a newly opened bag of sugar and a spoon.

"What's that for?"

"No idea. Antonio must have a good reason."

We stomped up the track to his sheds, only pausing every few minutes to re-wind our torches. Sadly they were on their last legs. We entered the badly illuminated shed. One solar light revealed Antonio standing next to a goat tied up to the food trough. He immediately gave orders.

"Diane, have you got the sugar?"

"Yes, nearly a whole packet. What do you—"

"Give it, give it," he said, cutting me off.

Pete and I shuffled over to him. We both took a sharp intake of breath. The poor girl had prolapsed. What should have been inside, was now outside. Next to her was a sleeping baby. Antonio poured the sugar over her prolapse.

"Why?" I asked.

"Sugar will stop it expanding. Pedro, we have to lift both back legs so that I can push it back inside her. You, Diane, will help me."

Medical Emergencies

Peter and Antonio lifted the poor goat's back legs so that she was now in a hand-stand position.

"Hold her legs tightly, Pedro. Diane, we have to push everything back inside. We have to be gentle and careful, but fast."

I sank my hands into the bucket of water he had placed by the medicine cabinet, which had some yellow liquid in it. I hesitated for a moment then got stuck in.

"When the goat stops trying to push it out, push it all inside."

I didn't understand until I was hands-on. No sooner had we pushed everything back inside than she pushed it out.

"We have to move faster, Diane. Once everything is inside, I have to put a couple of stitches in."

The poor girl in her hand-stand position was as confused as Pete, who in turn, was just about managing to hold her back legs in the air and avert his eyes from the business in hand.

She stopped pushing, and Antonio and I shoved everything in, as carefully as we could, but at the speed of light.

"Yeah," I said. "We did it."

It was then that the solar light went out.

"Shit, shit!" spat Antonio. "Okay, Diane. Keep your hand on her and push back as she pushes out."

I clamped my hand over her bits while Antonio grabbed my wind-up torch. He speedily wound it up then placed it in his mouth.

"Edro, et err eggs gown oly," he instructed.

"What's he saying?" Pete asked from the darkness.

"Let her legs down slowly," I translated.

As Pete gently lowered the goat's hind legs to the floor, Antonio's head started to bob up and down.

"Pete, take the torch from Antonio and wind it up," I again translated.

Pete extracted the torch from Antonio's mouth, wiped it on his shirt and wound it again. The light became brighter and Antonio leapt to his medicine box. He threaded the sutures and began to sew.

"More light Pedro," he said, as he secured a second stitch in place.

I still had my hand clamped onto her bits.

"She is not trying to push at all," I told him.

"She will be fine now," he said, snipping the last stitch. "Now she needs antibiotics and some of your special cream."

The special cream is pile ointment. I bought three tubes from the chemist who, when handing over the tubes, had a pained look in her eye. She held my hand for a few seconds when I gave her

Medical Emergencies

the money. I hadn't the heart to say, "It's for my goat's medicine box."

Pete and I walked back to the farm where I collected the cream and headed back up the track, leaving Pete to make some late supper and reheat the milky drinks.

On reaching the sheds, Antonio had given the goat antibiotics and a small feed. I handed over the cream and immediately turned to go back down the track. I was too tired to stay and chat. I needed a wash, supper and bed. Normally, on late-night runs to Antonio's, Monty would accompany me, but Katy had demanded a bedtime story and what Katy wants, Katy gets.

My wind-up torch was really on its last legs. My hand was forever trying to wind the blimmin' thing. I gave up and tottered down the narrow path in darkness. I tripped a few times, and then halfway down the path, something dug into my ankle. I quickly wound up the torch but could see nothing obvious and so I carried on walking. I reasoned that it couldn't be a sting from a scorpion, as by now I would be crying in pain.

I was tired and concentrated on not falling off the edge of the path. The pain got worse. Not a scorpion, not a snake. Snakes wouldn't be out at this time of the night, would they? Now my foot wouldn't work. I tried walking on tiptoe but the pain shot through my foot and up my leg. Maybe it was a baby scorpion? *Don't be ridiculous, Diane,* I argued with myself. I finally fell into our front door.

"Pete, I have a problem."

"No, no, no. No more problems tonight, Diane," he said, taking a bite out of his supper sandwich.

Paz immediately came to me and inspected my foot.

"You sit down, mum. I'll clean your foot, don't worry," her eyes told me.

I slumped onto a chair and let my cockney water dog sniff my foot and make a diagnosis. Pete couldn't ignore the problem any longer.

"You will need a torch, Pete. I think something has bitten me."

It's not that he didn't care, but some days, problems persist and sorting them gets a tad tedious.

"Move over Paz, let me look," he said, winding up his torch.

"She has got somefing stuck in her," Paz answered.

Focusing the torch on my ankle, he peered closely at the area that Paz had been licking.

"I think you have something stuck in your foot," he announced.

Paz shoved her nose into my hand, while Pete grabbed the tweezers.

"I can see something. It's like a tiny bit of twig. I am going to grab it and pull, hold tight."

I closed my eyes and Pete started to pull.

"Bloody hell, Pete," I winced, and held onto the sides of the chair.

"Bloody hell," echoed Pete.

"What, what?" I said.

"What, what?" said Paz.

"Don't look," said Pete.

I felt the tweezers tugging at something inside my foot and immediately, the image of John Hurt, the actor, laying on a table with the alien popping out of his chest flashed into my mind. Hunger and tiredness had overtaken my brain patterns.

"Look at this," said Pete.

Paz and I swivelled our heads to the kitchen table. I leant forward and Paz stood on her hind legs, front paws on the table, to examine the alien.

It was rather an anti-climax. On the table was a stick the length and width of a matchstick, end to end. Paz lost interest and climbed into her bed and went to sleep. Pete had already reached for the brandy bottle.

"That was horrible." His hand had a slight tremor.

"It's only a bloody stick, Pete, just a stick. All that drama for a stick."

"Diane, I had to pull that from your foot and it

is huge." He held the offending thing in front of my nose.

I had to agree. But after the two hours we had just experienced with Antonio, the stick was trivial and not worthy of a second glass of brandy.

"Well, this day in the office was probably one in a million," I said, splashing Betodine onto my foot. "We must buy some better torches though, just in case."

Two days later, Ruby went into labour. Ruby had developed bandy front legs. It may have been due to a lack of vitamins when she was born. Or it was her first pregnancy that buckled her legs, when she produced two huge boys. Who knows. But I wanted to be on hand to help her when she delivered this time.

She pushed and I pulled on her contractions and out popped a long baby boy.

"Well, done Ruby, here he is," I said, laying the kid in front of her nose.

I waited for the afterbirth to be delivered. Ruby grunted, pushed and everything came out. Yes, she had prolapsed.

"Pete! Sugar and phone Antonio!"

I grabbed the water bucket and sloshed water over her prolapse to keep it clean. Pete arrived with sugar and phone.

"Holy shit," he said. "I don't believe it!"

"No use turning into Victor Meldrew, Pour the

Medical Emergencies

sugar over it and phone Antonio. Tell him I need stitches NOW."

Thankfully, Antonio had arrived back at his sheds after taking his milk into town. He told Pete he would be down immediately, instructing him to grab some bailing twine.

Antonio arrived at the same time as Pete appeared with the ever-versatile string.

"Help!" I called, wide-eyed and scared.

This was Ruby, one of the first babies Antonio had given me to start off my herd. She was special to me.

"Okay, okay. She will be fine," he said, greeting me with a big smile.

Ruby was calmly cleaning her baby while Antonio looked for a place to lift her onto her front legs.

All three of us realised, at the same time, that Ruby's front legs were buckled

"She can't hold herself up on those legs, Antonio," I said, with my voice climbing two octaves higher.

"We solve problems, Diane, not make more!" he told me, and then took over.

"Pedro, move the baby to the fence, Ruby will follow. Diane, pick up everything from the floor and carefully walk with her."

We all shuffled into place.

"I'll lift her back legs and tie them to the fence.

You, Pedro, kneel underneath her to take the weight off of her front legs."

With Pete grunting somewhere beneath Ruby's front legs, Antonio and I went to work. He had already removed the afterbirth, and added more sugar. We pushed everything back in, lowered her legs and stitched her.

"Now we have a second problem," Antonio announced.

"What now?" I asked.

"As the baby suckles, she will push. You have to keep her upright and make sure she doesn't push. Otherwise, she will break the stitches and we will be back to square one."

He put the kid onto the milk bar and as soon as he suckled, Ruby began to push. Antonio clamped his hand over her bits.

"Roll me a ciggie, Diane," he asked, still grinning. "Twenty-four hours and she will be fine."

My mind went into overdrive, working out how one of us would have to stay with her for twenty-four hours with a hand clamped to her bits. Plus not allowing her to lie down.

"It is when she lies down that she will push," he said, his voice breaking into my thoughts. "I will walk your goats while you sort out, Ruby."

With that, he lit the roll-up, whistled my girls

Medical Emergencies

and strolled off towards the track, my goats in tow. They didn't look back!

And so the long day began. We took it in turns to hold Ruby's bits in place. Katy demanded her special food, *alamo*. Pete took off with the dogs and the little goat to cut branches for Ruby's tea. I was relieved of my duty to sort out food for humans, food for dogs, and food for horses. Pete was relieved to clean stables and set out food for the goats on their return. I was then relieved to set up the recovery stable for a long night with Ruby .

Ruby was exhausted. She lay down and immediately began to push. Plan D sprang into action. Pete lifted her and placed her over my legs. When I lost all feelings in both legs we changed places. In between this merry-go-round, we latched her baby on to feed. It was a long night, but finally, Ruby's urge to push vanished. As Pete and I fell out of the stable, at 6.30 am, both looking like Worzle Gummage, we were greeted by Antonio.

"How's the patient?" he asked, walking past us to examine Ruby. "Did you sleep here all night?"

"Yes," we answered in unison.

"You saved her. She will be fine now," he said, helping the baby boy onto Ruby's teat. "Give her antibiotics for three more days, just to be on the safe side."

As he left he called out over his shoulder, "I

have a youngster you may have to take on. I have named her Mikki and she has a problem. See you later."

Yet again he left us with our mouths open. We were too tired, dirty and hungry for further conversation. Tea and toast were made, and I dreamed of a power shower.

The rest of the day continued in a blurry haze. The dogs realised that their humans were in zombie mode and didn't demand breakfast. They just sat quietly, while I gathered the dog bowls. Katy, on the other hand, had no qualms in demanding her special breakfast. She ran around the kitchen, tea towels clamped in her mouth, jumping on and off the chairs. The dogs stared at her in horror. Paz stepped in.

"Get off the bleedin' chair, you 'orrible brat," she growled.

Katy, in defiance, leapt onto the kitchen table and tap-danced knowing she now had a captive audience. It was either laugh or cry. I laughed. Katy had broken my down-beat mood. Her humour became contagious. The dogs joined in. Martin found his ball, Monty and Rita Mae sat next to each other, cheering Katy on. Paz sat next to me and licked my hand. By the time I arrived at Antonio's sheds with the goats, my tiredness had disappeared, and my foggy brain had cleared.

"Where is this Mikki?" I asked him.

Medical Emergencies

Antonio emerged from the back of his shed, with a little brown goat draped over his shoulder.

"This is Mikki," he said.

"What's the matter with her?"

"We will walk to the Lost Garden, and you will see."

He and his goats left me in a cloud of dust as he took off at his usual fast pace, the goats having to trot to keep up with him. The Lost Garden had plenty of grazing to keep the goats happy for the afternoon. Antonio had decided that I was too tired to go further afield. I was a tad suspicious of this act of kindness. The goats always came first. His strict regime of hills, grass, hills, to finish the day's walk to ensure a balanced diet, was rarely compromised.

The little brown girl had been placed in the shade. She was about eight weeks old.

"Now tell me, what is wrong with her?"

"Not sure. She was okay when she was born but she has strange feet and now she can't walk."

He lifted Mikki and stood her on her four legs, encouraging her to take a step. She tried to take a step but her front legs were bent, and began to make a windmill action. One step and she fell over.

"I don't know if it's a problem with her brain or just a malformation of her legs. The first few weeks she was drinking and walking. I don't understand what has happened. You have to take her, Diane. She won't survive in the herd and her mother is too old to protect her. With you she has a chance to survive."

Stroking my ego does not work. I understood she would not survive with his herd. I understood Antonio had no time to take care of a special needs case as bad as this. He was appealing to my natural protective instincts, but, in truth wanted to help any disabled animal and knew that his friends would step up to the plate.

That evening he carried Mikki down to us, slung over his shoulders. Peter made a secure pen next to Ruby.

Over the next few months, Peter fell in love. He carried Mikki outside and taught her to drink from the big water bucket. He helped her to stand, and taught her how to walk.

"Mikki is an angel who has come to earth as a goat," Peter said, after supping his third small can of beer. "She is here to teach us stuff."

I humoured him by nodding and sliding a bowl of crisps over the table, hoping they would soak up some of the beer.

He was right of course. Mikki is an angel. She has taught us so much every day. She teaches us to be kind, humble, and brave and never to give up, no matter what life throws at us.

9

Cleft palates and cliffs

I sip my tea and stare up at Antonio's sheds. It's 5.30 am and the valley is quiet. There has been no contact from Antonio or his family. Pete joins me, his eyes barely open.

"No news is good news, Di. Why are we up so bloody early? We could have another half hour's kip."

"We may need to help milk his goats, so we have to get our lot done early."

"What's with the we? Your hand can't milk."

He sighs and walks back inside the house to pour another cup of tea.

He is right of course. My right hand is pretty useless after severing the tendon in my thumb. My left hand cramps from overuse, and both have a tendency to get stuck in a claw shape.

I help to tie up the goats that are waiting to be milked. Craning my neck to look out of the window, I check to see if Antonio's lights have been turned on.

"He is late, Peter. What on earth has happened?"

"You have become a curtain twitcher," he says, milking Susanna, who is objecting to having hands on her teats this early in the morning.

"Peter, get a grip. Antonio may be laid up. If so who will take over? Us?"

"Yeah, right," he mumbles as he wrestles with Susanna who is now Irish dancing.

"Lights are on!" I exclaim. "Lights are on!"

"Roger that, Diane. If we are needed, we will get a call."

The call comes at 9 am. It is Nacho, Antonio's brother-in-law.

"Pedro, can you help me with the goats?"

"Yes, of course. Is Agustin with you?"

"He is here, Pedro, but so much to do."

"Okay. I will be with you in half an hour."

Peter closes his phone and turns to me.

"So now we know. Antonio is not there."

"I'm coming up with you. I'll start sweeping up now."

We both step up a gear to finish our chores before heading up to the sheds. I enter with my stomach turning somersaults. Agustin is sitting on

Cleft palates and cliffs

Antonio's crate, milking at top speed. Nacho is sitting on another crate, trying to grapple with an indignant goat. Nacho is a big man, a policeman and all-round decent chap. He has no talent for milking but has a great deal of determination. Before Pete can take over milking the disgruntled goat, I kneel down in front of him to make eye contact.

"What's happened, Nacho?"

"He is in hospital," he says gently. "They have kept him in for tests."

"What do they think is wrong?"

"They don't know yet, we have to wait. But he will be fine, don't worry."

I know he is trying to reassure me that my friend is in good hands.

Peter suggests that Nacho takes a cigarette break while he (Pete) finishes off the goat. I turn to Agustin.

"What do you need?"

"Nothing, I'm good. Antonio will be back soon."

My phone rings.

"Diane, it's me," a familiar voice says.

"Antonio, how are you?"

Everyone in the shed stops milking.

"Tired, but the doctors are doing some tests. Don't know what they are testing for but never mind about that. Listen to me."

I relax to receive instructions.

"Show Agustin the walk to the second hill and Valencia. He needs to understand all the danger places, where the olives groves are. Give Penelope an antibiotic jab and feed her milk to the dogs."

I nod into the phone.

"I'll phone again later."

The call ends.

"The boss giving instructions?" Agustin asks with a smile.

Nacho looks at me with inquiring eyes. I shrug in reply and tie up Penelope Cruz, preparing to administer antibiotics. I write Penny's tag number and date on the chalkboard but also decide to spray a silver spot on her back so no mistakes can be made. It is time to leave the men to their work. After instructing Agustin to meet me at the bridge at 2 pm, I wander slowly back home, hoping Antonio will phone me later and tell me what really is going on.

When we first discovered that Katy had a cleft palate, I immediately sought advice on the many American goat-farming websites. I prefer American sites because we share so many similarities. They are off-grid and in the middle of nowhere with limited access to goat vets. Over the

Cleft palates and cliffs

weeks I had many replies which, although informative, gave me little hope that Katy would survive. Except for one.

A lady messaged me at length on how to manage my little girl with correct feed and vitamins. But she added a word of caution. She told me that she had lost her cleft palate girl when she re-introduced her into the herd. She was bashed by one of the others and broke her back. Her bones were not strong enough to withstand the everyday pushing and shoving within the herd. I thanked her for the advice and noted that she may have saved Katy's life.

I considered letting her play in the paddock with the young goats, to slowly wean her off the dogs. Monty loves her, but she demands all of his attention. Rita Mae tries to deflect her away from the ever-patient mastin by storytelling.

I marvelled at Rita's ability to settle Katy at bedtime with tales of the *campo*. But it was unfair that all the working dogs had her to deal with after a long day.

"We have to make a better plan for Katy," I told Pete, as we tried to relax for an hour after a long hot day. Katy was dashing in and out of the house, tea towels in her mouth, having snatched them off the kitchen counter. Monty and Rita Mae were snoozing in peace next door, leaving

Martin to clap and cheer her every move. Paz and Lulu pretended to be in a deep sleep.

"Diane, for God's sake, she gets two walks a day and food on demand. What more can we do?"

"We have to help Monty. We need to tire her out at night. You need to play football with her, then play the guitar to soothe her."

Pete opened and closed his mouth, goldfish-like, but no words escaped. I grabbed the opportunity to take advantage of his stunned silence.

"Right, I will fetch your guitar. Try and soothe her while I collect the tea towels from the yard. With a fixed smile on my face, I handed him his guitar. Pete walked outside, pulled up two chairs and began to strum. Katy stopped twirling and jumped onto the other chair. She was enchanted.

"What are you thinking?" I said to Pete, as he launched into AC/DC's *Highway to hell*. "We don't want her head banging!"

He switched to *La Bamba*.

I shook my head. He scowled at me and Katy began to tap dance on the chair as I walked back into the house.

Moments later I could hear the gentle tones of *Irene goodnight Irene, Irene goodnight*. I peeped out the door to see Katy lying down on the chair, resting her head on the arm. Then, minutes later Peter

Cleft palates and cliffs

carried her into the feed shed and placed her next to Monty and Rita Mae. My plan had worked.

"Can we stop now, or do I have to serenade the whole herd?"

I handed him a beer and we sat down at the kitchen table in silence. Two minutes later we were both humming *Irene goodnight Irene, Irene goodnight.*

🐾 🐾 🐾

Birthing was over and the girls couldn't wait to escape from their kids and walk free in the *campo*. The rains had stopped and bridges had been repaired. Antonio decided to take the route to the mill with his herd, but I wanted to keep a little closer to home. The girls needed a rest, not only from their babies, but from hours of cross-country hiking. Let's be honest. I, too, was tired. I grabbed at any excuse not to tramp for miles with Antonio barking orders at me.

It was hunting season, so I thought it prudent to leave Monty at home. He has a dislike for hunters. For his (and their) safety, he would have to remain on a lead for the whole afternoon. I, too, have a dislike of hunters, but I don't pack the same bite as my big mastin. Paz needed a day off and as she was snuggled with Martin by the wood burner, I did not feel guilty leaving her behind.

Rita Mae wanted a break from Katy and was ready to go. Chinni's teat was bad again and so Pete was providing meals on wheels. Thankfully, I had Carmen the sheep to look after me and the herd.

It was a beautiful day, bright with clear blue skies. I had my wellington boots on, as the ground was a little muddy, but all in all it was a perfect afternoon. We headed off to the bridge, which Pete and Antonio had repaired a week earlier, and climbed up the first hill. The goats were enjoying the herbs, and for an hour, we gently zig-zagged the well-trodden goat paths. I should have continued meandering up and down the hill, but no, I had a bright idea. My girl, Paz, would have been surprised.

"Could be dangerous, Mum, what you finking?" she would have asked. "That's wot I do best."

However, Paz was at home and not able to keep me in check.

Rita Mae, on the other hand, loved days like this, when her elders were left behind and it was just the two of us. Although Rita had been labelled the intellectual member of the family, she liked to break out and have adventures. I spotted, in the distance, a very green and bushy piece of land, just by Antonio's 'long green'.

Cleft palates and cliffs

"Look Rita, over there. That looks perfect for the girls."

Rita swivelled her head in the direction that I'd pointed.

"I can't understand why Antonio hasn't used that bit of grazing," I commented.

Carmen also looked to where I was pointing and mumbled something under her breath, which I didn't quite hear. Rita gathered the goats and we all headed to the narrow path close to the lush green that I was determined the girls should enjoy.

"Come along, girls. Climb down to the five-star restaurant."

I had a rather smug smile on my face. For once, it was I who had found wonderful grazing, not El Maestro. The goats climbed down from the path and began filling their tummies with green bush. Carmen remained on the path.

"Come on, Carmen," I called to her, as I climbed into the wooded area. "It's great down here."

"You idiot," she baa'd, quite loudly.

I am quite used to Carmen's views on my competence and mostly she is correct. But today I replied, "Okay, righto," and continued to climb down into the wonderful wood, full of old olive trees and bracken. A few paces in and I realised why Carmen had called me an idiot.

The area was full of rocks and huge boulders

covered in moss. The ground was steep and very slippery. My brain seemed to go into slow motion. I looked up from the treacherous ground to see my goats leaping back onto the track. Looking back down again my slow brain began to register that the land sloped towards a cliff. Below the cliff were rocks and water.

The words *holy crap* entered my slow thoughts, just as my feet started to slide away from me. I looked up again to see Carmen ushering the herd back to the hill, with Rita Mae keeping them in a straight line. I fell onto my front and my life turned into a scene from *Romancing the Stone*. I was on a rollercoaster ride towards a cliff edge.

I grabbed at tree roots but they all came away in my hand. I looked up. The ridiculous notion that my great mastin would magically appear to save me, crossed my mind. But all I saw was Loretta, the sheep with little or no brain. She, too, was on the rollercoaster ride to the cliff edge. If the impending fall didn't maim me, the sheep would. Another huge bush that I tried to hold on to was torn out of the ground.

Suddenly, my feet hit a big boulder, and I came to an abrupt halt. Alongside was a dense bush that Loretta slammed into. Thankfully it held her weight.

I carefully crawled over to her. I reached into my rucksack to retrieve the collar and lead that I

Cleft palates and cliffs

always packed in case of emergencies. Loretta was in shock but remained calm. I was confident that Carmen and Rita would take care of the herd, so I just had to work out how to climb back up to the path with a fat sheep in tow.

Loretta and I remained on our knees as I led her left to a denser part of the wooded area. I figured if we slipped again, the bushes would hold both of us. I hauled Loretta up and we fought our way through bracken, bushes and undergrowth. Finally, I could see the path above me. I pulled myself up the bank, hands resting on the path, ready to heave myself, and Loretta, to safety. My eyes made contact with a pair of boots.

I looked up. Towering above me was a hunter, decked out in camouflage gear. I scrambled up and hauled Loretta onto the path. I removed her collar, and she immediately ran off to join the grazing herd.

I took a deep breath and in my poshest Margot Leadbetter voice (a character from the British sitcom, *The Good Life*) said, "Good afternoon."

I left to catch up with the girls, leaving the poor man with his mouth open. To this day I wonder how he described events to his friends in the bar.

My relationship with cliffs has always been tricky. I slid down one on my back because I paid more attention to my phone than where I should have been placing my feet. I climbed a cliff to rescue a puppy (Rita Mae). The top stones came away in my hand and I dived into a damp (thankfully) river bed. At another time I got stuck trying to cross a cliff face, stones falling on my head. The conclusion my animal friends (and husband) have come to is that I am a bloody liability and definitely not good on my feet.

I try to be careful and, most of the time, avoid *campo* dangers well. That was until one summer afternoon when I made the decision to walk the girls on land close to our farm. Yes, it was illegal, but my quiet, gentle dog, Rita Mae, the family lawyer, told me it would be okay as the neighbour's four cows grazed on our land most afternoons.

So, although the cows were eating the horse food, the goats would be eating the bush and herbs that the cows didn't eat. All in all, in Rita's opinion, we were good to go. I left Monty and Paz at home. Both dogs were feeling the heat and their age. Antonio thought I mollycoddled them but I felt that they should relax. They had earned semi-retirement. They could walk with Katy and Martin and be relieved of the responsibility of looking after Mother.

Cleft palates and cliffs

Rita and I herded the goats into the dry river bed so that they could eat cane in the cool while we waited for the cows to climb over the broken fence and eat on our river banks. The sound of the cow bells alerted Rita that they were on their way. She slowly pushed the girls out of the river bed and as the cows jumped onto our land, we jumped into theirs. The cows waved their huge horns at us in greeting and we nodded to them in reply. Everything was going well with the goats enjoying the herbs and bushes.

We made our way upward. I walked with the special needs goats on a tiny path that the mountain goats used to reach the river. Rita Mae kept an eye on the rest of the herd which was higher up. Our narrow path ran along a cliff edge that fell away to the rocky riverbed below. I needed to be careful but could afford to daydream about new fencing and glass in the windows at home. Then something spooked the goats above.

Rita flew to my side and, with the girls hot on her heels, I was surrounded by hysterical goats. A wild boar must have been grazing high in the bushes and scared the poor dears. I was buffeted on all sides as they pushed past me to get to the narrow path. All I remember is being pushed over the edge of the cliff.

Later, Pete thought I must have knocked myself out on landing, and that's why I have no memory of falling. That makes sense, but the odd thing is, below the cliff, there were huge boulders and rocks. There would have been a lot of blood had I bashed my head. But somehow I managed to miss the boulders. I believe an unseen hand caught me and gently placed me on the sand between the boulders, which is where I woke up.

My eyes shot open and I concluded that I had fallen. Now I had to assess the damage. I peered down at my legs to check for protruding bones or blood. All good. Next, I wiggled my toes. Yes, they were working and so were my hands. I tried to roll over but I felt sick. Phone, phone. Where the heck was my phone? I remembered that it was in my shirt pocket . I grabbed it and I still don't know how I made the call.

"Peter. Middle Beach. Help," was all I could say.

We had named parts of the river, Bay of Pigs, Middle Beach and Jurassic Park. Pete arrived, panting and frightened.

"What the hell have you done? I think I'll call an ambulance. Let's get you sitting up. No, wait, that could be dangerous."

I tell him with huge smile, "Toes are moving, no pain in my back. I think I am just winded. I'm alright. Go to the goats. Rita Mae is with them. I'll catch you up."

Pete is not convinced but he knows well

Cleft palates and cliffs

enough that I hate being fussed over. If I was in real trouble, I would tell him. Left alone, I slowly swivel onto my knees and crawl over to where my stick has fallen. With the help of my trusty walking stick, I stand up. *Brilliant,* I thought, and took a step forward. I phone Pete.

"Houston, we have a problem."

"What, what?" his voice sounds as if one of the goats has headbutted him in his nether regions.

"Not sure, nothing too serious. Just get the girls back to the paddock with Rita Mae and grab another walking stick."

As Rita and Pete gathered the goats, I gathered the courage to try to put weight on my right foot again. Pain shot through me. I peered down. In truth, my eyesight is pretty bad, and I couldn't see if my foot was swollen or if my toes were broken. I was stuck and I really needed the loo. Thankfully Pete arrived in record time with the extra walking stick. With his help, I hopped back to the house. Paz and Monty waited in the doorway.

"Wot you gone and done, Mum?" asked my little cockney water dog.

"One minute, everyone, I need to spend a penny."

With Pete's help, I managed to get to the loo

with my dignity intact. He then helped me back into the house.

"Come and sit down, Mummy," Monty said in his Prince Charles voice, walking ahead of me, guiding me to my chair.

Pete filled the washing-up bowl with water and ice cubes. I gingerly lowered my foot into the icy water.

Peter knelt down to examine my foot.

"You must have broken a bone. It's all puffy."

"No, I don't think so. I've only bashed it. In a few days it will be okay. Now, where are Katy, Rita and Martin?"

"Rita and Martin are babysitting Katy and I'm glad you're that confident it will only take a few days to heal."

His thoughts were the same as mine. One man down at the farm is a nightmare.

It actually took nearly two weeks for me to be able to walk the goats. Our dear friend, Anne Marie, put out a *Help Pete and Di* message, and amazing friends cooked meals for us. The amount of practical help we received really humbled us. We have been so lucky and now, when I walk past the cliff and look up at the distance I fell, it amazes me. It cements my belief that the universe takes care of us and that angels, in human and spiritual form, are real.

10

Fast responses

I am hoping to receive another phone call from Antonio for an update but so far, nothing. Agustin is waiting by the little bridge with the herd.

"Hi, has Antonio phoned you?" I ask.

"Yes, he said he is fine and that I will be milking for a while."

I feel a little put out that he hasn't phoned me. But that's Antonio!

"Okay, let's go. And pay attention."

I sound rather stern but I need to establish my authority, at least until Antonio returns. I keep up a steady pace to reach the first feeding stop. I show Agustin the danger places and where there are holes in the fence on the neighbour's land. Also a small parcel of land where new olives have been planted. I have to admit that I thought Agustin would not pay much attention. But I am surprised how much he listens while managing the goats and dogs too. As we settle down to eat late lunch, my phone rings. It's Antonio.

"Are you out?"

"Yes, of course. Everything is fine. What's happening?"

"They are moving me to Malaga hospital tomorrow, for more tests."

"How are you feeling, Antonio?"

"Me, oh I'm fine."

"Okay, that's good. Agustin is doing well and the dogs and goats are happy."

"Got to go," he says.

I can hear the voices of his wife and (I assume) doctors in the background. I now know that my friend is in big trouble. I have to keep everything together, especially with Agustin who is now likely to play a bigger role in Antonio's affairs. We pass over a ditch into a flat, scrubby area and I take the opportunity to tell him the story of Antonio and the drunk hunters.

※ ※ ※

Take the pebble from my hand," Antonio instructed.

Fast responses

"Oh no. Have you been watching *Kung Fu* last night?"

It was a very chilly afternoon and Antonio decided to keep us all warm by going on a good hill hike. He had also decided on the afternoon's entertainment. On the palm of his extended hand was a small stone.

"When," he said, with a huge grin, "you can take the pebble from my hand, Grasshopper, you can call yourself a goat herder."

The game commenced. I spent the next hour trying to snatch the pebble and losing. Antonio, like a dog playing fetch, does not tire of this game. We hear a few guns blasting away in the distance. I left Monty at home because of this. Rita Mae also needed a day off and so my trusty Paz had joined us. Her arthritis was escalating, and I had to take care to balance her love of work with the exercise needed to do it.

"Try again, Diane. Come on," Antonio urged. "You can do it."

I made another feeble attempt and was met with a closed hand. Antonio's mastins began to bark loudly. He dropped the pebble and squinted into the distance.

"What is it, Antonio?"

"Hunters. We had better get to the front of the herd before the dogs get into trouble."

I hung back and watched Antonio approach

two hunters who were standing around a little fire pit. I heard Antonio quieten down his dogs as he walked over to them. Paz stayed firmly by my side.

"Don't like the look of 'em, Mum," she said with her eyes.

"Me neither," I agreed.

It seemed the goats felt the same. They dashed past Antonio and the hunters to eat on the land a little away from them.

"Who are you? What's your name?" asked one of the hunters.

I detected a slight slur and spied a bottle of gin lying on the ground. I walked up to Antonio.

"Don't answer," I hissed into his ear. "They are drunk."

"Come here and have a drink," said the hunter.

"No, no. I'm fine," replied Antonio, and began to walk towards the herd.

"Come on. Have a little drink with us and we can talk about who we know in Olvera," said the hunter, holding up the gin bottle.

Antonio doesn't drink except on special occasions like weddings or Christmas. Until today.

"What are you doing?" I asked as he started to walk over to them.

"One little drink and they will be happy," he replied.

I stayed put and looked down at Paz. Then

Fast responses

both of us stared at Antonio approaching the hunters.

They had come well-equipped. They handed Antonio a small shot glass and filled it with gin. He knocked it back in one and it was quickly filled again.

"Hey lady, come and have a drink with us," the taller of the hunters called over to me.

"I think not," I replied in my best Margot Leadbetter voice. I am sure it didn't have the same impact in Spanish.

Antonio began to glug the second shot of gin.

"Antonio, I'll take the goats to the next hill. You can catch us up." I was still in Margot voice mode.

"I won't be long," he said, a large grin sweeping over his reddening face.

"He won't be long," the hunters echoed and began to laugh.

Paz and I stomped off with our noses in the air. I called the two herds, and headed towards the next hill. Thankfully Antonio's dogs came with me and helped Paz round up all the girls. I think they were as disappointed in Antonio as I was.

We descended the hill, crossed a track and made for home. There was still no sign of El Maestro. I decided to phone him.

"Are you coming or not? I am taking the herd home now."

The hunters began to laugh in the background.

"I'll come when I'm ready," he slurred.

"You tell her, blondie," his new friends shouted in the background.

Antonio disconnected. Paz rushed to my side when the swearing began.

"Let's go 'ome, mum"

"Yes Paz, let's go home."

We set off. Fifteen minutes later the phone rang. It was Antonio. I declined the call. He phoned three more times. On the third I answered.

"Sod off!" I said, and disconnected.

He tried a few more times to contact me but I ignored his calls. We were half an hour away from home. The goats were munching on grass and bushes beside an *arroyo* (gully), when Antonio appeared behind me, barely able to stand. Of course, I stated the blimmin' obvious.

"You are drunk!"

"I only had a little *copita* (glass)," he slurred, holding up his forefinger and thumb to show me how little he had drunk.

I stared at him.

"Honestly, I swear I'm fine," he said, clutching onto an olive tree to keep his balance.

I walked away and he tottered after me.

"Why are you so mad? Why didn't you answer

Fast responses

your phone? A ranger told me the route you had taken." He was trying hard to sound sober.

I turned swiftly, which startled him, and he made an attempt to clutch at a bush to steady himself.

"First, why are your clothes muddy? Second, those men could have robbed you. We don't know them, and you acted like an idiot." I spoke slowly, to let my words seep into his drunken brain.

"I rolled down the big hill. I tripped up and just rolled. It was easier and quicker. And don't be ridiculous, those men couldn't have robbed me!" He tried to sound indignant but failed.

"Really! They couldn't have robbed you?" At speed, I poked him on his chest. He fell back, landing on his backside.

My point had been made and now damage control was needed. I hauled him to his feet.

"Check your wallet," I instructed.

He did and assured me that all was in order. I handed him my water bottle and made him drink. Next, I fished a packet of mints out of my rucksack.

"Start sucking these to disguise the smell on your breath. Chari will go mad if she gets a sniff of gin."

We finally made it back to his sheds. My goats dashed off down the path for home and tea, with Paz on their heels. I turned to Antonio.

"Don't you ever do that again. Do you understand?"

"Okay, okay. But honestly, it was only one *copita*," he said, smiling.

I turned for home. I too smiled, happy in the knowledge that tomorrow, my friend would have the mother of all hangovers.

※ ※ ※

Antonio and I quarrelled, normally within five minutes of meeting up. It's the little things. Where are we walking in the afternoon? Who last had the hoof trimmers? Whose turn is it to buy medicine? What name should be given to his young macho/chicken/snake? After about half an hour, we settled down to our favourite films, Spanish versus English proverbs, and Spanish versus English insults. It took two days before Antonio understood a line from the film *The Outlaw Josey Wales*. We both love Clint Eastwood films.

"Best insult, Antonio: *Don't piss down my back and tell me it's raining.*"

"Don't understand, Diane."

I repeated it, he squinted then shook his head. After two days of repeating this insult, I almost gave up. Finally, the penny dropped and he agreed that Clint had the best insult and was in the best films.

Fast responses

Antonio was firmly in charge when we walked, and yes, it drove me crazy. But whatever bad situation we found ourselves in, he took over and sorted it out quickly and calmly. I thanked the Lord that he was at hand when Chinni was being strangled to death.

Antonio had moved to his summer residence, the Molino, and we'd met up in the beautiful spot we call the Canyon. It is my favourite place to graze the goats, although it does hold a host of memories. I'm reminded of a dangerous flash flood and how we survived almost being crushed by a boulder avalanche Also my rather stunning recovery from a cliff fall into the damp river bed. Apart from these little mishaps, the Canyon has little rock pools, where boots can be taken off and feet cooled. The goats can take a nap in a cool wood and eat the lush foliage that grows on the sides of the river banks.

Antonio had phoned me in the morning to make sure I had put my boys saddles/aprons on. His machos had started getting frisky, and we didn't want mating to begin just yet. Antonio fashions the saddles from a thick piece of rubber, an old car seatbelt and rope. The rubber is placed underneath the buck's tummy, and the seatbelt is tied exactly like a girth on the boy's back. The rope is attached to the side of the rubber, which, in turn, is tied to another rope. This is placed around the buck's neck like a collar. A saddle with neck and side reins, just upside down. The boys may get a bit frisky with the girls but with the saddles on, there are no worries of early pregnancies.

By the time I arrived at the Canyon, Antonio was lying on his log bed, hat over his face and snoring loudly. His bucks were fighting each other and running around, sniffing at all the goats. Chinni was not amused when Bruce Lee trotted up to her with amorous overtones. Chinni's impressive horns were lowered to hook Bruce's leg. They ducked and dived, rearing and twisting around each other. My girl was definitely not in the mood for flirting.

Unlike Alice, who was strutting her stuff in front of Julio and Brad Pitt doing her best Mae West impersonation. My laughter at Alice turned into a scream when I looked back to watch Chinni. She had hooked her horns underneath Bruce Lee's neck strap and side reins. Bruce swivelled, and Chinni was being strangled and dragged. She was totally helpless.

"Antonio, MOVE!" I screamed, while running up to the entangled goats.

I tried to relieve the tension on Chinni's neck,

Fast responses

but it was too tight. Her eyes were bulging and her tongue was hanging out. Antonio arrived at my shoulder and in a flash his sharp pen knife began sawing through the rope. It took seconds to release her. Chinni fell to the floor, and I fell with her. I held her in my arms and rubbed her neck. Antonio fetched his water bottle and moistened her mouth.

After five minutes my darling girl had regained her strength and stood up. I guided her to a rock pool and watched her drink while Antonio repaired Bruce Lee's saddle. I was very shaken. Those seconds, watching my girl choking to death, kept going round and round in my head.

A shadow blocked out the sun. It was Antonio, standing in front of me rolling a cigarette.

"Thank you, thank you. She nearly died," I said.

"Yes, she did. So the moral of this story, Diane, is what?"

I stared at him blankly.

"Diane, the moral of this story is to always carry a knife and keep it sharp. One day I won't be here to come to the rescue," he said quietly. "I've told you. Always be prepared and train your brain to think fast."

It was Chinni's daughter, Ivy, who made me engage my brain really fast.

Ivy is as beautiful as her mother, being tall and graceful. Sadly she did not inherit her mother's brain. I likened her to a highly strung, thoroughbred racehorse. When we set off for a walk, Ivy would sometimes run blindly in front of the herd. Chinni and I never worried as within a few minutes, she would return in a panic to the middle of the herd. We would all shake our heads and carry on.

One time, she refused to leave the farm for nearly six months. She had a complete nervous breakdown. Pete had to feed her, along with the other special needs goats, while giving her one-to-one counselling. This continued until she felt confident enough to rejoin the herd.

This particular afternoon, I decided not to walk to the Mill to meet up with Antonio. It was hot and sticky, and I was tired. I took the girls to one of Antonio's old groves, which was not too far from the river and home. Paz and Monty came with me, leaving Rita and Martin to babysit Katy.

Staying close to home meant that the special needs goats, and sheep, could also have time out in the *campo*. With Paz and Monty looking out for the herd and the specials I could, hopefully, relax and daydream of affording a new roof on our house. I was pulled out of this fantasy by

Fast responses

Paz's barking, and Monty standing in front of me.

"What's going on?" I asked Monty, wildly looking around the herd.

I then saw one of my girls in immediate danger.

To reach the leaves, the most agile of my goats had jumped into the low branches of the olive trees, while others were standing on their hind legs. Ivy had stood on a bank and reached up for the higher leaves. She had placed both legs on a branch to steady herself, but one leg had slipped and got trapped between two branches. Her back legs were teetering on the edge of the bank. She was now, literally, being crucified. One slip…

I leapt into action, ducking beneath her to take her weight on my back but that wouldn't free her leg. The branch was too thick for me to break and it would take too long to climb the tree to reach it. Ivy's breathing was accelerating. What would Antonio do? He would focus. Problem: hoof jammed in tall branch. Goat too high and too heavy to lift. Goat is going to suffocate. Solution: volleyball.

My hand-eye coordination is rubbish. Tennis, badminton and ping pong are beyond me. I have never played volleyball but that is what I had to do now. I needed to punch her hoof out of the branch. I ran from underneath her teetering body, stood in front of her, bent my knees, and leapt into the air. I pulled my arm back, fist clenched, and POW, I delivered a powerful punch onto her hoof. It worked. Her hoof popped out of the branch vice.

I fell to the ground and Ivy fell on top of me. For a few minutes, goat and middle-aged lady grunted and swore. Ivy eventually scrambled off me and limped over to the herd, who were standing and sharing a large cone of popcorn while watching the spectacle. Paz and Monty rushed to me, anticipating giving me the kiss of life and/or cardiopulmonary resuscitation. Neither was needed. I stood up and checked my knuckles. They were blooded and skinned.

My phone rang.

"Diane, can you drop the antibiotics off at my house tomorrow lunchtime?" Antonio asked.

"Yes, okay. About 12.30?"

"That's fine. Is all good with you?"

"All good, just a typical afternoon."

There are times when achievements, great and small, are best kept to oneself. Because, as soon as you speak of them, the moment disappears. I wanted to savour this one for a while.

11

A trek

We are on our way to visit Antonio in Malaga Hospital. I have always been a bad traveller and motorways really scare me. Although I have a map on my lap, I am holding my breath and squeezing my eyes shut. Peter is relying on me for directions. We have yet to work out how to put Google maps into our phones.

"You can't read the bloody map with your eyes closed, Diane," he snarls.

"And you know how scared I am driving on a motorway," I snap back.

The squabbling begins.

"Oh, so I am a bad driver. Is that what you are saying?"

"Don't be ridiculous. Oh look, there's the hospital!"

"So now you open your eyes just when we've passed the turn-off!"

"Now what?" I am exasperated now, mostly with myself.

"I'll get us there. I'll just follow my nose." His tone is slightly calmer.

Peter's nose is as good as Alice's. She can smell an opened packet of peanuts half a kilometre away. I knew we would get to the hospital in time for Visitors' Hour.

In truth, it had been a long morning. To be able to get away from the farm to visit Antonio, we had a ton to organise. The alarm had gone off at 5 am, which allowed us to get ahead with milking and other chores. Pete had dashed up to the sheds to help Agustin with his milking. We fed the goats olive cuttings that Pete and I had collected the previous evening. The horses had an early lunch. We then washed, dressed and headed into town to drop off our milk at the cheese factory, before setting off for Malaga.

We pull into the hospital car park and I reach for my phone to call Antonio.

"We are here," I tell him.

"I'm on floor 3, room 218." He sounds very cheerful.

I follow Peter along corridors and up stairs to

A trek

floor 3. Antonio is outside his room and waves to us. It's a bit of a shock to see my friend standing in blue pyjamas. I see how vulnerable he looks. Chari, his wife, ushers us into his room and we make awkward conversation.

"He has his own bathroom," says Chari.

"Marvellous," I reply, beaming.

I admire the bed, the décor and the small balcony with views of distant mountains.

"Come look at the view, Diane," says Antonio, his eyes wide.

I take this invitation to mean that he needs to talk 'goat'. I leave Pete to chat to Chari while Antonio and I slide out the door to stand on the tiny balcony.

"Every afternoon I can see goats coming down the hill. I can hear the bells," he tells me.

He is looking into the distance, smiling. I follow his gaze and wonder how he could see goats so far away, let alone hear bells. I say nothing.

"How is everything in Las Vicarias?"

"Your goats are fine," I tell him but quickly add, "they are missing you, and the dogs are missing you too."

He smiles and sits on a little stool that has been dragged out onto the tiny space.

"How are you, my friend?" I ask. "What is happening? Why are you still here?"

"I'm okay. I don't sleep all the time. I've had the big machine look at my head."

I assume the big machine is an MRI scan.

"What has the doctor said?"

I try to sound firm wanting him to give me a proper answer.

"Oh, they said I have a small speck thing in my head and they will take it out."

A blood clot or a tumour? I wonder. I am still reading between the lines.

"When are they going to operate?"

"Not sure, maybe a few weeks time. I have to stay here for a while so they can check me." There is a tiny hint of concern in his voice.

"Best you are here rather than in Olvera," I say with a reassuring smile. "So don't worry."

I look into the room and catch Peter's eye. I am hoping he has managed to extract more information from Chari.

"We best go inside. Don't want you getting cold out here."

"Okay, but I really am fine," he says, as we walk back into the room. "I keep my muscles working don't I, Chari?"

Chari rolls her eyes and ushers Antonio to lie on the bed.

"He is driving me mad," she says. "He keeps lifting water bottles up and down." She

A trek

demonstrates her husband's weightlifting technique.

"I have to keep my muscles strong," he says quietly.

"I understand that," Chari counters, "but you are doing press-ups too. That can't be good."

"I have an idea," I interrupt. "You need squeeze-balls to keep your hands and arms strong."

I am not sure how my squeeze-balls translate into Spanish as Chari looks bewildered. But Antonio is not and he understands.

"Chari, later on you have to go to the shops and find two (unintelligible words) balls," he instructs.

Before she can answer, he turns to me and bombards me with a flurry of questions about the goats, following up with a blizzard of instructions to pass on to Agustin. When he finally draws breath, he politely asks, "When is Felicity coming over?"

"Soon Antonio, soon," I tell him.

We walk back to the car, deep in thought. We sit and fiddle with our seat belts. I break the silence.

"What do you think?"

"He looks much better. Chari said he can have the operation and he will be fine."

"I need to know more, Pete."

"It's not our business. We have to keep out of it and just look after his herd until he's back."

He starts the car and I let my mind wander to places I have been trying to avoid for the past week.

"You are right. We'll keep his girls going. He will be back. Summer is just around the corner."

※ ※ ※

Before the summer heat arrived, Antonio moved his herd upriver to his summer residence, the Molino. The mill was now a semi-ruin, situated close to the river, surrounded by huge eucalyptus trees. It had been in the family for many years and Antonio told me stories of when he was a young boy. How he discovered the hiding place in the chimney where his aunties kept wine and spirits, only to be retrieved on special occasions.

Antonio was convinced that his lack of enthusiasm for alcohol stemmed from sipping gin and wine when his family were sleeping. Only to be found drunk and sick a few hours later by an irate family member.

He showed me where a beautiful rose garden was planted and the big stone wall that was built to protect the house and garden. Now, the eucalyptus trees had goats sleeping under them, and the rose garden was the cool area where the

A trek

dogs slept. The hiding place by the old fire now held Antonio's lunch, safe from dogs, goats, mice, and the odd snake.

In the early years, when I was building up the herd, my girls would stay at the mill with Antonio's goats. The special needs goats and the two sheep stayed with me at home, while the rest of the girls enjoyed 'summer camp'. We made a separate corral for a few of my goats to sleep in. Antonio felt that Alice, Susanne and Willow would start fights between the two herds. He was right of course. Those three could start an argument in a hundred-acre field full of lush grass.

Summer camp was fun for our goats, but a lot of extra work for us. Most of the herd had dried up as they were pregnant, but some still needed topping off. Antonio would milk and Pete, who had to drive from our farm to the mill, left the car at the head of a track leading down to the mill. He then walked for fifteen minutes down the bumpy track to the mill sheds. He helped carry the different milk churns into Antonio's Land Rover, sweep up and check our girls.

Meanwhile, I fed the animals that were left behind at our farm, prepared the evening food, and did the washing. The list of chores went on. At midday I would hike, in the blazing heat, over to the mill, ready to walk the goats in the afternoon.

The normal routine was as follows. On arrival, I dived into the mill to cool down, then checked my girls, shoved a banana into Alice's demanding mouth, and waited for Antonio to arrive.

Most afternoons we would keep close to the mill or walk over to the Canyon. But this particular year, there had been little spring rain, and summer grazing was sparse.

"I have a plan," Antonio told me, as he climbed out of his Land Rover.

"Oh no," I said, half under my breath.

"We need to walk the goats to Salado. My brother said that there is lots of food over there."

Antonio's brother, Gabriel, manages a large estate on the north side of Olvera. It's a mixed farm estate of cattle and arable ground.

"Don't be ridiculous. We would have to walk for an hour or so to get there. Plus we will have to walk through part of the town!"

"Trust me, it will be good for the goats. So tomorrow, be here at eleven o'clock and we will get there before it's too hot."

He said this with a smile that said *end of conversation*.

As I prepared my rucksack for the day's work, Paz, obviously worried when I told her of the day's plan and that she and Monty would be left behind, sat in front of me.

A trek

"Sounds bleedin' dodgy to me, Mum," she said in her cockney voice.

I bent down to reassure her that I would be fine. She called for back up and Monty appeared.

"Mummy," he said, in his Prince Charles voice.

"Monty," I answered him, as he placed his nose in my hand. "I will be very careful on the road, and if you stay home you can help Pa."

Both dogs blinked and walked off. They had given up offering their dumb human any further advice, resigned to picking up the pieces at the end of the day.

I arrived at the Molino at 11 am. Antonio had already gathered the goats. His rucksack was on his back.

"Let's go," he said, full of enthusiasm.

"Hang on, I've just arrived, I need ten minutes to sit down."

"No time for that. Let's go."

The first half hour was spent climbing up the steep track to the overhead road bridge. We took ten minutes to sit in the shade before marching on up the track that had olives on either side. The dogs had to work hard keeping the goats in line. I was knackered and we had only just begun the trek to Salado.

Antonio slowed the goats down and waved to me to catch up with him. I made a feeble attempt to jog, looking more like a drunk trying to walk in a straight line.

"I'll stay in front, you keep at the back. Make sure the goats keep walking. Don't let them stop until we get to the top car park. Watch out for fast bikes and cars."

All I could manage was a salute. My mouth was dry and my brain was already addled from the heat, which seemed to be getting more intense by the minute.

I adjusted my straw hat, took a deep breath and we began the next leg of our journey. The goats huddled together as we marched along the road. Luckily there were few cars, as we were close to siesta time.

Four middle-aged farmers stood outside a large garage to watch the parade. They nodded to Antonio, smiled at the goats and sniggered when I walked past. To be fair, they saw a tall, blonde English woman trying to look like a professional goat herder. I stuck my nose in the air and prayed I didn't trip up.

All was going well until we reached the top of the road and turned into the car park, by the upper cemetery. Alice and Felicity decided they wanted to walk down the cemetery path to examine the flowers.

"Get back up here," I snarled.

A trek

"NO," they both shouted and began munching on a hedge.

Antonio was now out of sight, walking the herd down towards the road we had to cross, taking all the dogs with him. Why, oh why, had I left Paz at home? If I ran towards them, they would go into toddler mode and run further away. Help came in the form of a beer can that was in the middle of the car park. I grabbed the can and threw it in the direction of the two goats. It bounced loudly on the path and rolled into Alice's legs. It had the desired effect. They both screamed and ran back to me.

We jogged to catch up with the herd. Just as I thought the drama was over I saw Julio, Antonio's large horned buck, enter a building where cookery classes were taking place. Three seconds later the screams began. Antonio halted the herd.

"Julio is starting trouble," I shouted to Antonio and pointed to the door the boy had entered.

"GET HIM!" he shouted back. "FAST!"

As I arrived at the door, Julio trotted out, followed by ladies waving tea towels. Instead of re-joining the herd, Julio trotted into an open garage doorway followed by the tea-towel-waving ladies. He came out, cantering this time, as an elderly lady, brandishing a broom, had joined the tea towel wavers. I stood, mouth open, the Benny Hill theme tune swimming in my head.

"Diane, get him under control NOW!" Antonio shouted.

"JULIO," I shouted. "Stop it, you shit!"

Buck, tea towel wavers and broom brandisher stopped dead in their tracks. I walked up to Julio and gave him the look. He lowered his head and walked to the herd. Alice was in hysterics, as were Antonio's girls.

I turned to the ladies.

"I am very sorry. He is young. What can I say?"

I gave the Andalucian shrug, left them blinking and caught up with the herd.

"Now we cross the road," said Antonio, Julio's antics forgotten.

The road we had to cross was the squiggly busy road, leading to the main part of the town.

"Oh dear God," I said, partially under my breath.

I have a huge fear of traffic around animals and I could feel my heart rate increasing.

"Don't worry. I'll stop the traffic and you lead everyone across," he told me.

The goats were getting impatient. Antonio strode into the middle of the road and waved me across.

Alice sensed my fear, and followed me at full speed. The rest of my goats followed at the same velocity. Antonio's girls walked calmly

A trek

across the road with his dogs trotting on either side.

"Come on, we have to get going and find the girls food," Antonio said, striding past me.

My nerves were still in recovery.

"No wonder your goats are neurotic," he said as he gave me a withering look over his shoulder.

I thought that remark was a tad harsh, and the following year I would show Antonio how calm my goats could be .

We finally arrived at his brother's *cortijo*, which was situated by the side of a well-maintained track. The goats dashed across the river bed to rest beneath a huge grove of eucalyptus trees. On the other side of the road was about fifty acres of barley stubble plus twenty acres of hills, scrub and herbs. A goat's five-star restaurant.

At around 5 pm we headed for home. It was all uphill, and I was very tired. My water supply was almost empty and hot. Antonio handed me an orange to suck. Although it relieved my dry mouth, the orange came with a few problems. Wasps and biting flies swarmed around my head. I give thanks to the invention of wet-wipes and cheap fly spray. I sucked, wiped, sprayed and fretted about crossing the road again.

"Hold the herd here, while I stop the traffic. I'll call and you bring them across slowly. I repeat, slowly," Antonio instructed.

Of course, I ignored him and called my girls together for the dash.

"Slowly Diane. It will make the cars slow down," he shouted.

"Bollocks," I shouted back.

We made it back to the mill in one piece. I ignored the farm workers who were still sniggering outside the huge garage, as I walked past. I tried to ignore my burning feet, that had been rammed into my boots since 5 am. But I couldn't ignore the fact that I would have to do the same again the following day, and possibly five more.

After settling the goats, Antonio and I drove back up the track to the top road where Pete was waiting for me. I was so tired I could barely talk. Thankfully, I had made a huge cheese-and-bacon pie the day before so dinner was sorted. My head hit the pillow and I knew no more until the alarm went off at 5 am.

I survived the next seven days and the farm workers stopped sniggering after day three. By Day Six, they tipped their hats and said, "Good afternoon". I would like to say I had won their respect as a goat herder but I think they applauded the English woman's staying power.

Working with Antonio, I didn't have much choice.

12

Salado

I am standing at Malaga Airport Arrivals, waiting for my youngest daughter, Felicity, to come through. The morning had started with a few hiccups. The horses had broken their fence and pottered upriver. It took half an hour to find them and an hour to bring them back home. Peter had already given the goat's alfalfa and sugar beet. I arrived home with the horses following me, looking guilty.

With no time to repair fences, we locked the equines in a smaller paddock, gave them breakfast and prayed they wouldn't wreck the paddock before we got back from Malaga.

The journey down to the airport is uneventful, meaning I keep my eyes closed most of the time and Peter sings loudly. I vow every journey to relax, but the vows are always broken. For me, the one-and-half-hour trip is like sitting in a dentist's waiting room, preparing to be called in for a root canal filling.

Fliss strides through the doors, rucksack on her back. Her beaming smile erases the dentist trauma.

"Are we going to visit Antonio?" she asks.

"Would you mind making the detour?" I ask. "You've had a long morning."

"Don't be ridiculous, Mother. We're here, let's do it."

We arrive at the car. Pete and Fliss hug and we climb inside.

"Shall we visit Antonio now we are in Malaga?" I ask Pete.

"Yes, but I have to work out how to get to the hospital from here. Pass me the map."

"Just tap the name of the hospital into the phone, Pete," says Fliss.

"Eh?" we both reply.

Fliss stares at the oldies, inhales deeply, whips out her phone and takes over.

"Name of hospital?" she asks.

I tell her and she taps the info into her phone.

"Right, Mum, swap places so I'm in front with Pete. We'll be there in about fifteen minutes."

An American lady is now barking directions at

Pete, guiding him towards the hospital. I phone Chari to tell her we are on the way.

Antonio is, again, waiting for us in the corridor outside his room.

"Feliz! Feliz!" he calls to my daughter.

Fliss hugs him, and I see she is fighting back tears. Like us, it was the first time she had seen El Maestro so vulnerable. We sit in his room, his wife chatting so fast and non-stop that we have difficulty understanding. I catch Antonio's eye. I need to talk to him. I need information.

"He should be in bed," says Chari, hoping I can persuade her husband to rest.

"I have to keep my muscles working."

"Plenty of time to get fit after your operation," I tell him. "When is it?"

"Exactly. Now, back in bed or you may have another 'thing'," says Chari.

My head whips around to meet Antonio's eyes again.

"What thing?" I ask him.

"I have lots of medicine to take. The operation is in a few days time and I'll be fine." He follows this with the *end of conversation* look.

The remaining half hour is spent talking goats. I can see how tired he is, and sense that talking is demanding a great effort.

We take our leave, wishing him well. I promise

to call but, more importantly, to take care of the goats. Chari races after us as we head to the lifts.

"I need you to pick up Agustin in the morning and get him to the sheds," she says.

"What?"

"Pick him up at 5.30 am," she says, and returns to Antonio's room.

Fliss, yet again, takes over. She knows how busy and tired Pete and I are, plus having the worry for our friend.

"I'll pick Agustin up in the mornings and I can help walk the goats. Problem solved. Now, let's go and buy some wine and a take-away for tonight. No cooking."

We spend the journey home talking about Antonio and come to the conclusion that the man is a survivor. He will get through this. We can't work out what the 'thing' is, Maybe a seizure? We just have to hold the fort until he comes home.

Salado raises its ugly head again. That sounds harsh. Salado is pretty and has much grazing for the goats. Unfortunately, the year before, it also meant hours of walking across town, up and down steep tracks, all in the blazing heat of the midday sun.

On arrival, the goats rested for twenty

Salado

minutes, and then we stood in the heat as they ate. When they'd had their fill, at around 6 pm, we walked all the way back to the Molino, now in the sticky evening heat. I swore never to do it again.

"I have a plan," said Antonio, on my arrival at the Molino.

"A plan for what?"

"Salado."

"I am not walking there every day. You can, but my girls are not!"

"I have a plan," he repeated.

"Okay, I'll play. What is your plan?"

"I'm fencing the eucalyptus grove and they can sleep there."

"That's the plan? They will be scared and vulnerable."

"My plan is to sleep there with them for a few nights making sure they are happy. And besides, they have Luna and Cheeta to protect them."

"And milking?"

"They are mostly dried up and I can milk them at the grove, no problem." He smiled. He knew he had my attention. "I'll make a separate place for your lot. Now, tell Pedro that on Sunday, we fence."

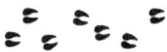

The late June heat arrived. Pete and Antonio prepared the grove at Salado for the goats' summer holidays. The following day, they moved the feeding troughs and then the huge water trough.

That afternoon we walked the herds to Salado. Alice, Patty and Pepa staked out the best spots in their corral. The rest of the girls followed suit and bagged their own beds. The only goat that didn't want to enter the 'Las Vicarias' corral was Hildegard, who preferred to stay with her mother, La Tahona.

Hildy is the gentlest goat in my herd. She is tall, cream in colour and has magnificent horns. We named her firstborn Vinnie, after Pete's Aunt Lavinia. Hildy adored Vinnie, and loved to show her off to her mother. Antonio gave me Hildy when La Tahona had given birth to triplets. He felt two were enough for the older goat to take care of, and he wanted me to have this prize baby to build up my herd.

Hildy, although bottle-fed by me, never forgot her mother. She always ran to greet her mum when we walked with Antonio's herd but after saying goodnight to her, she was happy to leave and come home with me. Now, Hildy and her daughter had the opportunity to spend this summer vacation with grandma.

We walked the goats gently downriver. Both

goat herders and goats were tired and couldn't face the blazing heat in the big field. Pete and Chari were at the corrals when we returned. They were unloading a garden lounger, sleeping bag and food, in preparation for Antonio's two nights sleeping with the herd. Chari wanted him to come home for a shower and a hot meal. He didn't want to leave the goats until they were used to sleeping outside under the stars.

The following day, at 1 pm, I drove to the grove and found Antonio asleep on top of his Land Rover. His hat was covering his face and he was snoring, as was his companion, Manoli, who was snuggled into him. I checked my girls who were enjoying a siesta. Antonio had walked them for an hour after milking.

"Oi, time to wake up," I called to the top of the Land Rover.

Antonio removed his hat from his face and tried to sit up but his faithful young goat was still deep in slumber.

"Manoli, you have to wake up now," he told the brown bundle.

Slowly Manoli roused herself and followed Antonio down from the Land Rover roof.

"How did you sleep last night?" I asked.

"Oh, it was great," he said, with a big smile. "The dogs slept around me and the goats were close by. Best night's sleep I've had for years."

"Why were you sleeping on top of the Land Rover and not on the lounger?"

"Because the other goats wanted to sleep next to me and it got hot. I climbed onto the roof to get away from them, but Manoli jumped up, and I got tired of pushing her down."

I could tell that Antonio was really enjoying this time with the animals. He loved the fact that they wanted to be next to him. One of his favourite films is *Dr Doolittle* and, in his mind, he is the Spanish version.

"Right, come on. We go downriver today and liberate some melons," he said.

I was still puzzling why melons needed liberating when Antonio opened the corral gate and the goats took off. My herd stayed close to me. Alice looked fed up, and her best friend, Pepa, kept close to her in order to keep Alice's baby, Patty, under control.

Patty adored her mum and loved jumping on and off her back when they lay down. When walking, Patty found logs to jump on, hill mounds to run up and down, screaming, *wheeeeeee* and encouraging the other babies to join in the fun. Alice was not amused. She needed to be in control of every situation. Patty was not a naughty baby, just an energetic one.

We walked on tracks and sandy paths, keeping

close to the river. It was all new to me, but not to Antonio.

"Keep walking the goats on this path. I'll be back in a few minutes."

He disappeared behind some trees and I thought he must have needed a pee. Five minutes later he caught up with us and pointed at his rucksack, which was bulging.

"Melon has been liberated," he announced.

The penny dropped and I asked no questions. We stopped alongside a shady path, right next to the river. The goats drank and settled down for a rest. Alice found a spot away from the herd to relax but Patty had other ideas. She bounced on and off her mother's back.

Antonio released a huge melon from his rucksack and began to cut it into slices. Alice raised her head when she smelt the fresh melon but Patty jumped on her and she lowered her head, defeated. Patty was her first baby and the experience of motherhood had been quite a shock.

Pepa came to her rescue. Antonio and I tucked into the melon and watched as Pepa swapped places with her friend, allowing Alice to sneak away and sit next to us to share the fruit.

"Look, look," said Antonio, pointing at Pepa.

The tall, black, beautiful girl had laid down and allowed Patty to fall asleep on her teats.

"She is a good friend to you, Alice," said Antonio, passing her a portion of melon.

Alice and I looked over at Pepa and little Patty, both now asleep. I think Alice knew how special her friend was. She was always by Alice's side, ready to protect her when she overstepped the mark and got into a fight that she couldn't win.

Pepa was well-respected in both herds. Not only was she loved for her kindness, but her boxing skills were truly admirable. She was hornless but that is an advantage in a boxing match. Horned goats limit their moves, only using them to disable their opponent. Pepa used her height, agility, weight, and quick thinking to overpower her opponent. Also, she never looked for trouble, only protecting weaker goats or babies and, of course, Alice. Together they are Butch Cassidy (Alice) and The Sundance Kid (Pepa). I loved them both.

Antonio continued, all afternoon, to show me the danger points. There were fruit and veg gardens hidden behind tall bushes and thick bracken. The owners accessed their gardens from a higher track so there was no way of knowing what was hiding behind the hedgerows. It was all new to me and the dogs. By the time we all arrived back at the corrals, we were exhausted. Antonio hadn't stopped barking out directions and orders during the entire walk.

"It's important, Diane. We can't make a mistake with the goats over here."

"I know, but this is all new to me and the dogs are trying their best."

"Oh yes, the dogs. Cheeta is doing so well." He pointed at Monty's daughter. "Last night, Luna slept next to me, but Cheeta stayed in the middle of the herd. She is a good guardian. I think she will be the best I have ever had."

"I'll tell Monty."

I climbed into my car. It was getting dark and I still had lots to do at the farm.

"I have a new plan for tomorrow, Diane. If you get here by 11 am, I can go and have breakfast and a shower."

I arrived promptly at 11 am. Antonio was in the middle of the huge field with all the goats. The dogs ran to greet me.

"Keep them grazing, Diane, and don't let them go to the high hill. Just let them graze here. The dogs will help you."

He was clearly tired so I just saluted and took up my post, cowboy hat pulled firmly down to shade my eyes and my trusty walking stick to lean on.

After an hour, I was wilting, and so were the girls. The midday sun blazed down and the dogs had found shade under an olive tree, close to the no-go area. I felt my concentration going. It was then that I saw Lee Van Cleef.

I stared into the distance, and all of a sudden, the land ahead of me became blurred. A heat haze. Out of the haze came a galloping horse with Lee Van Cleef mounted on top. I knew it was him from his black hat. I hoped he would pull up his steed before he ran into the goats and scattered them. The sound of a harmonica came from my left.

Am I on the film set of *Once Upon a Time in the West*? Am I going mad? I watched as the goats ran towards the harmonica player. Mr Van Cleef seemed to have raced off in another direction and disappeared.

"Diane, Diane, what are you doing?" a familiar voice called.

The harmonica player was Antonio, who had whistled the goats. I staggered to the track, found El Maestro and sank to the ground.

Antonio grabbed my hat, ran to the river, filled it with water and tipped it over my head. At that moment his brother, Gabriel, walked up.

He shook his head and muttered, "Idiot." I am not sure if he was addressing me or Antonio.

"Need anything?" he said.

"No, we are fine," Antonio said, I thought a tad prematurely.

"Okay," Gabriel said, and strode away.

The cold water over my head had done the trick. For two minutes I spewed out one long sentence, full of English swear words. Antonio just smiled.

"You are feeling better?"

"You are an absolute bastard. You and your brother."

I was now almost crying. Pitiful I know.

"Why, What?"

"Gabriel just asked YOU if I needed anything. YOU said no without speaking to ME and then, and then, he walked off!"

"You're just overheated. Sit in the shade for the afternoon, I'll sort out the goats. Next time, bring the goats to the trees; don't just stand in the field."

Yet again he leaves me speechless. It's always my fault and on reflection, it was. I was following orders but they were stupid orders, and that will not happen again.

I still walked the goats in the heat, but at noon, I brought them back to the corrals.

Mad dogs and this Englishwoman will stay out of the midday sun.

13

Flash floods and Philip

It is the day of Antonio's operation. When I spoke to him last night he sounded a little drowsy but resigned, accepting this inconvenience as temporary. In fact, he was more worried about his goats and that Choo (Two) and Manoli were missing him. I choose my words carefully and tell him that, of course, they miss him and he has to get better quickly.

Agustin is doing very well. His hands and arms, however, are aching, having to hand-milk so many goats. Antonio's brother-in-law, Nacho, helps when he can, as does his father-in-law. But the weight of managing the herd is on Agustin's shoulders. I administer any drugs that are needed and keep the medicine board up to date.

Fliss has been getting up at 5 am to be in town

at 5.30 am to pick up Agustin. No problem for Fliss, who is always up feeding her horses and mucking out stables before work in the UK. It is Agustin's habit of lighting up a joint that annoys her. She makes him stand outside the car to finish smoking before climbing in, which Agustin can't understand. They argue with each other in their own languages before setting off to the farm.

Today I want peace and time with my daughter, as she is leaving in the morning. I decide to let Agustin walk Antonio's herd upriver without me. Fliss and I will keep my girls at home. The weather has been unpredictable this month with storms, hail, wind and sunshine. It has been tiring second-guessing what the afternoons have in store for us. The route I give Agustin is easy and will keep the goats away from any danger. Fliss and I take all the dogs with us as we potter around our land. The goats settle down to eat in the olive grove and we sit on a log to watch.

"Mum, Paz is very stiff."

"I know, Fliss." My eyes fill with tears.

"I heard you get up to carry her to the toilet last night."

"I know, Fliss."

"Mum, I think…"

"I know, Fliss."

Flash floods and Philip

Our time in Salado had been fairly uneventful so far. The goats had plenty of food to keep them happy. While they were eating in the huge field, I thought I could catch up with my reading. Antonio had other ideas.

"It's *honda* (slingshot) practice time," he announces.

"I can't use a *honda*. You know that."

"We all have to keep practising. You may have improved."

Having nearly taken Antonio's eye out in my last attempt to use the slingshot, I was told never to pick one up again. Antonio appeared to have forgotten this and placed a stone in the sling. I twirled it as instructed.

"Now release, Diane."

I released and again the stone shot backwards, not forwards, failing to hit the innocent olive tree that was the target. Three of Antonio's dogs saw the stone whizz past just above their heads. He took the *honda* from my hand.

"Not much improvement, Diane. My turn."

The next hour was spent with me providing stones for him to hit the trunk and limbs of the poor olive tree. Antonio was a good shot. He had to be when we walked into people's olive groves. The girls were permitted to eat the herbs and grasses surrounding the trees, but he had to maintain discipline. We needed the goats to keep their heads down for an hour, without a tree being touched. And that's when Antonio's skills were needed.

When a goat reached up to munch on an olive branch, Antonio slung a stone at the tree. The noise of stone hitting wood deterred the goat. His accuracy was, to me, astounding. Directing the dogs to control the goats in this situation was effective but they tended to scatter the herd.

After an hour of practice, Antonio decided we should walk high on the hill, to allow the girls to eat the herbs. This was all new territory to me and my girls stayed close. They seemed a little nervous. We zig-zagged higher and higher. I was enjoying the view but Antonio was watching the skies.

"There is a storm somewhere over there," he said, waving his hand in the direction of Seville.

"That won't affect us, will it?"

"It might." He sniffed the air.

Half an hour later we heard a distant clap of thunder.

"Time to get back," he said.

It seemed to take forever to walk down the narrow hill paths to reach the river crossing to the corrals. We heard crashing sounds long before we reached the bottom track.

"Flash flood, Diane. We are in trouble."

Two tractors, two jeeps and six farmworkers were gathered on the track, gazing at the river. I

Flash floods and Philip

held the goats in the big field while Antonio assessed the problem.

"We won't be crossing over to the corrals for at least two hours. Come and look."

I walked over, leaving the dogs in charge of the herd. The gently flowing river that ran between the eucalyptus grove and the track, had tripled in size. Cane, logs and debris rushed past. I stood, mouth open, watching nature's spectacle.

"We will be here until midnight," Antonio said, reaching for his phone. "Make the call to Pedro. I'll phone home."

We all sat on the warm track for two hours, waiting for the river to subside to a safe level so the goats could cross. The men didn't stop talking the whole time. I was hungry and needed a shower. The goats had come down from the field and two hundred lay on the track around the chattering men. Finally, Antonio decided we should try and cross.

"I'm not wading into the river. Think of another plan," I told him.

"I have a plan, Diane. I'll drive the tractor. You sit in the bucket at the back and call the goats. Your lot will follow you."

He was very confident and jumped into his tractor as I moved the farm workers out of the way.

"Don't scare the goats. Do not touch them or the mastins will bite your balls off," I told them.

I had to be firm as *campo* men like to interfere. I thought that, if I scared them enough, they may do as I say. I climbed into the bucket on the back of the tractor and called Pepa. My big black girl walked towards me with Alice hot on her heels. The rest of my herd stood up and followed.

"Okay, Pepa, we have to get across. Be brave and follow me," I told her.

Antonio slowly drove the tractor into the river. I kept talking to Pepa as she waded in. Alice hesitated then did a huge leap, landing next to the bucket, drenching me and her friend. One by one my girls walked into the river. Antonio drove the tractor slowly to the other side, climbed out and whistled his goats.

The dogs sprang into action, carefully pushing their charges. The mastins walked by their sides, giving them confidence. Thankfully, no testicles dangled from their jaws. Pepa led my herd up the bank to dry land and I walked them to the corral. Steadily, all Antonio's goats crossed, following the Las Vicarias Ladies.

After settling everyone down and feeding the dogs, we finally left at midnight. The bridges we had to drive over, to get to Olvera, were being cleared of debris by the farm workers. I climbed

Flash floods and Philip

into my car, started the engine and just as I was pulling away Antonio appeared at the window.

"Well done, Diane. Your goats led my herd over."

"Las Vicarias goats are very intelligent, Antonio."

"Yes, they are. You can learn a lot from them," he said, a huge grin on his face.

Yet again, he giveth and he taketh away.

In *Feria* week everything closed down. Everyone was on holiday, except us. We tried to attend at least one evening of celebrations. It took us a few days to recover. We went straight from *Feria* to work. We avoided speech, heavy lifting and making big decisions. Whatever happened to those days when we could dance all night, go to work and feel fine after a twenty-minute power nap?

We attended one night of *Feria,* and the noise was so loud we gave up on conversation. The best part was eating *churros* and hot chocolate at 5 am with our friend, Elma. We could actually engage in conversation. There was a nip in the air. The weather was on the change.

Antonio had instructed me to meet him at his house at midday. He was walking the goats for a few hours in the morning and so I was excused the 11 am walk. Pete needed the car to collect animal feed and drove me to Antonio's house. As I climbed into Antonio's Land Rover we heard the first clap of thunder. He crunched the gears and the old Land Rover leapt into action.

"We should be able to get across the bridges and to the corral, before the river gets too big," he shouted over the roar of the engine.

We raced to Salado, taking bends at a velocity I would never have attempted. The first bridge was clear of water but the river beneath was flowing fast. There was one more small bridge over an *arroyo* (stream). I closed my eyes because Antonio was pushing the Land Rover to its limit.

Suddenly the brakes were slammed on and I was thrown into the dashboard.

"Shit. Too late."

I opened my eyes and saw the river raging over and under the small bridge. Without a word, he made a three-point turn and hurried back to the first bridge. Again I was thrown into the dashboard but this time my eyes were wide open. The main bridge had disappeared and the river was flowing fast over it.

"Now what?" I shouted.

Antonio didn't answer. He did another three-point turn and stopped the Land Rover halfway between the two bridges.

Flash floods and Philip

"Now what?" I repeated.

"I have to get to the goats. There are babies there and this time the river could enter the corral."

He climbed onto the Land Rover's roof and reached for his phone.

"What's your plan?"

"I'm phoning Nacho. He could climb down the hills from the other side and get the goats to safety."

I heard him bark orders to his brother-in-law while pacing around the roof of the truck. He waited ten minutes, rolled a cigarette and paced some more.

"Is Nacho coming?"

"Yes. He is climbing down the far track with a friend. But it will take too long."

He paced some more, then climbed down off the roof.

"I can't see what's happening. I have to get closer. Follow me."

I climbed out of the Land Rover and trotted behind him to the second bridge. Boulders and debris were being thrown up from the *arroyo* below. Antonio walked along the bank to the narrowest part. The river was racing.

"I think I could jump across."

"Antonio! You are joking!"

"No, no. One good leap and we will be on the

other side. Then I can see what is happening to the goats."

He walked away to get a good run at it.

"Follow me."

He ran then leapt into the air and landed cleanly on the other side. He didn't look back.

I made the same leap. I fell on all fours and looked behind me, to see the river throwing up more stones and branches.

"Dear God, thank you," I muttered to myself.

I caught up with Antonio who was pacing up and down the river banks, watching for Nacho.

"There he is," I said, pointing to a figure in the distance.

For the next hour, Antonio and Nacho yelled at each other across the river while I sat and read my book. Farm workers finally arrived from downriver to clear the bridges, and Antonio collected his vehicle. After another half an hour we put the Land Rover into four-wheel drive and crossed over to the herds.

The river had entered the corral, but had now subsided. All the animals were fine. Nacho and his friend got a lift back to Olvera while Antonio and I walked the goats in the old grove.

Antonio was fussing over his girls and I fumed. By the end of the day, when all the goats were put to bed, dogs and babies fed, Antonio could no longer endure my silence.

Flash floods and Philip

"What is the matter with you?" he asked, a tad loudly I thought.

"You didn't look back!"

🐾 🐾 🐾

It had been a wet winter. I kept my girls close to home because Antonio was again walking his herd by the road. The girls were enjoying being rested after days of walking over hills. Rita Mae was excellent, helping me keep the goats away from the neighbours' olives. She needed no instructions, she understood her job. It allowed me time to enjoy daydreaming about new fencing and a new roof, and a barn full of hay and a shed full of logs. I was interrupted by my chirping phone. It was Antonio.

"I need the anti-inflammatory, thank you."

"I'll bring the bottle up this evening."

"Good," he said, and disconnected.

That evening I placed the dumplings I had prepared earlier into the stew pot and wearily trudged up the path to Antonio's sheds. After he injected a goat with the medicine, I turned to leave.

"Wait, wait. I have something to show you."

I could almost smell the dumplings bubbling away in the big stew pot. I was so close.

"Okay, show me."

He walked to his small shed, beckoning me to follow. I entered and saw three Spanish water dog puppies.

"Look, look," he said, kneeling down.

"Oh, how sweet! I didn't realise you had puppies up here."

"No, I didn't want to say anything just yet. I thought I had homes for all three of them, but one pup is perfect for you."

"Eh?"

"Watch."

He placed all the pups in a row and walked away. Two jumped towards Antonio but the third quietly waddled towards him and sat. He then gave them some goats' milk. Again, two pups dived into the bowl but the third quietly waited until his siblings had calmed down. He then waddled over to drink.

"Is he a bit slow?"

"No, Diane, he is perfect," he said. "I would keep this boy but I have too many dogs. So you must have him."

"I can't have another dog. End of conversation, Antonio."

"Diane, Paz won't be able to climb hillsides like she used to so you need another hill dog. This one will be the right one for you."

"Pete will go mad."

"Logic, Diane, logic. You need a young dog and this is the one I would choose."

I looked at the little black pup, picked him up and cuddled him.

"He is lovely. But I failed to train Rita to be a hill dog. What do I do with this one?"

"Easy, Diane. Paz will teach him," he said confidently. "While she can still work, let her teach him. She is the best."

My brain was racing. Antonio's logic was spot on. But how do I tell Pete we have another mouth to feed? I cuddled the pup tightly to me.

"Oh, and he has a name."

"You have named him already?"

"Yes. His name is Felipe, after my old dog. He looks just like him. He can't come down to you for a few more weeks, so you have time to prepare."

I realised that the deal was done. All I had to do was convince Pete (and our animal family) that Felipe should come and live with us. I prepared myself for a long night.

Three weeks later I carried the little boy home. Peter hadn't taken as much convincing as I thought, having seen the logic in Antonio's argument. I wouldn't get Paz's full reaction until the puppy entered the house. I had spent every evening visiting Felipe, so he would get used to my smell, and now we were at our front door. This little black bundle's new life was about to begin.

The dogs could smell the puppy under my coat. They shook their heads and, except for Paz, settled back down to sleep.

"Wot you got there, Mum?"

"He is all yours, Paz. You are in charge of this boy. His name is Felipe."

Peter had hauled the old rabbit cage into the house so Felipe could have his own secure bed. We placed toys and little food bowls inside.

"Shall we put him straight into his new bed?" Pete asked.

"No, I'm giving him to Paz. She will take over from here."

"Are you sure?" Pete was stroking the pup, who was now snuggled into my neck. "She may not take to him, you know how she can be."

"Quite sure, don't worry."

I placed the pup in the middle of the floor. He waddled over to my slippers and Paz growled.

"Diane?"

"It's okay, just watch."

He waddled over to my rucksack. Paz growled. She continued to growl every time he touched anything of mine that I had left on the floor. Until he found the rabbit hutch. As he wobbled into his new house, Paz went over and gave him two licks, then walked away.

"You just leave him to me, Mum. I'll 'ave him

in order, don't you worry," my little girl told me with her eyes.

Paz was happy for me to pet and cuddle Philip (on Paz's orders, we now reverted to the English way of saying his name), but in everything else, she was in charge. She showed him where to go to the toilet outside, not to touch the older dogs' bones and not to chew my shoelaces. I marvelled at her ability to keep the young puppy under control. Only when Philip had learned the rules of the house did Paz play with him. Play was his reward for getting things right. The other dogs walked around him, Martin walked next to him and Paz enjoyed being his mentor.

Philip

Over the next two months, Philip would join the dogs, and Katy, on their early morning walks. It amazed me how Monty and Martin would patiently watch over Katy, as Paz educated Philip about the dangers of the *campo*. This would allow me, Lulu and Rita to enjoy early morning time together in peace.

The new routine that Paz had clearly set out for us was for Rita and I to take the goats out for their walk, bringing them back via the hill at the back of the house. I would then bring Rita home, collect Paz and Philip and run back up the hill to the goats.

Paz would take over again, showing Philip how to calmly walk up the hill to get above the goats and watch them. As the goats made their way down the hill for home, Paz taught Philip to check that all the goats had come down, before showing him how to keep them together. He followed all her instructions, taking his new job very seriously.

It astonished me how Paz explained everything so clearly, and how she remained calm if he got something wrong. Paz, not noted for her patience, seemed to have an abundance with Philip. She gave him confidence. She showed him how to deal with tricky girls like Alice and Willow. She showed him how to read the herd.

Over the following months Philip got faster and stronger, now leaving Paz at the bottom. She was satisfied that Philip was now equipped to go

Flash floods and Philip

further and become as good a hill dog as she was. Paz then handed him over to me.

"All yours, Mum, don't muck him up. I can't climb them bloomin' hills no more," she told me, in her cockney voice. Her eyes were telling me that her joints were hurting a little more.

My eyes filled up watching her struggle to walk down the path for home.

"Don't worry, Mum, old age catches up on all of us," she told me later, as I helped her onto her soft bed. Monty lay next to her. Two old friends together.

14

Jonathan

Antonio stays in hospital for two weeks after his operation. He has been home now for four days and today we are paying him a visit.

"What can we take him?" Peter asks. "Oh wait, I have an idea. We have *Kung Fu* videos, remember? He will like those."

"Good idea. I'm taking bailing twine."

"Bailing twine? That's not much of a welcome home present."

"Trust me."

We park the car and walk to Antonio's garage, carrying our presents in plastic bags. He opens the door and I take in the huge scar along the side of his head.

"Hello, friends. Yes, I look like Frankenstein," he smiles and points at the wound.

Peter steps forward and gives him the bag of videos. He is pleased and shakes Pete's hand.

"Thank you, thank you."

I step forward and hand him a bag full of black bailing twine. For a second I wonder if I have made a mistake. But only for a second. He opens the bag and a huge grin spreads across his face.

"Perfect," he announces, pulling the long twine from the plastic bag.

Bailing twine, to a farmer, is an essential piece of equipment. I learned how to twirl two pieces together to make collars for the goats and to give gate latches extra strength. My rucksack is held together by twine. Most of my fences are too. I even repaired Bailey's head collar with the stuff.

Antonio begins twirling with a huge smile.

"How are you?" I ask.

"Me? Oh I'm fine. I am going to see the goats tomorrow."

"You are taking it easy," says Chari, who appears at the door. "And sorting him out."

"Him?" I ask Antonio.

"Bernado. Here he is." Antonio kneels down by his tractor which is parked inside the enormous garage.

Jonathan

A huge puppy, looking like a St. Bernard, appears from behind the tractor.

"This is Bernado. He was given to me and he is coming to meet the goats this week."

"Good. About time he went to live in the *campo*," Chari says. "He keeps shitting in here."

"What do you expect?" Antonio says rather sternly. "He is still a baby."

Bernado leapt back onto his bed behind the tractor as Antonio took up twirling his bailing twine again.

"He is going to be a big boy," Antonio says to us, looking at the pup on his makeshift bed. "And yes, I'll sort him!" he shouts up the internal staircase at his retreating wife.

Time for us to leave.

"I'm going to sit in the Lost Garden tomorrow afternoon and wait for Agustin to bring the goats home," he says, walking us to the door. "I want to surprise them."

I smile. He looks like a little boy on Christmas Eve.

"How are things with you?" he asks. "Is Felipe doing good work?"

"All is well, Antonio, all is well," I tell him. "Philip is brilliant."

"I told you Paz would teach him. She is a very good dog."

"She is, Antonio. Paz did a very good job." Peter puts his arm around me.

We say our goodbyes and we leave, promising to meet him at the Lost Garden tomorrow afternoon. Peter and I had decided not to tell him that our darling Paz had crossed Rainbow Bridge two days earlier.

Our special needs unit was growing. Coco, our gentle brown and white girl, had lost the plot. Her sense of direction was non-existent and walking with the herd became quite tricky. If she stayed in the middle of the herd, she was safe. But take your eye off her for a minute and she'd disappear.

Coco had been retired for a year before we knew something was wrong. We retired her because every year she had difficult births and always triplets. Luck was with her as Antonio was at hand to deliver the babies, until one November night.

It was birthing time and we were very tired. This year, Alice, Welfi and Sandra needed extra care and help with their babies. Peter was making new pens as fast as the goats were delivering. Coco went into labour at 10 pm. Antonio's lights were still on, so I rang him.

"Coco is in labour."

Jonathan

"Is she pushing?"

"No, not yet, but she is groaning a lot."

"As soon as she pushes, go in and get the first one out and all should go well. I'll be here for a while. Joanne is taking her time and Penelope needs some help."

"Okay, and good luck."

I felt a little better knowing he would still be in his sheds for a while.

I must be the only person who works with goats that dreads birthing time. Antonio barely copes but he loves the challenge and loves the babies. I, on the other hand, am in a state of anxiety the whole birthing period. The girls depend on me for help and I can't let them down. When dealing with Antonio's goats, I am calm and collected. When it comes to my own, I haven't got to the place where I can be detached and not show my concern.

I was helping Willow's baby to latch on when I heard Coco cry. Pete and I rushed to her side. She started to push, stopped, and cried. I immediately phoned Antonio.

"I think she is in trouble again, Antonio."

"I can't get down yet," he grunted. "I'm trying to help Penelope dilate."

"What should I do with Coco?"

"Diane, for goodness sake go in and see what the problem is. Alright, Penny, don't push yet."

Pete held the phone while I washed my hands. Then I went in.

"It's a breach, Antonio," I shouted into the phone.

"Find one back leg," he said calmly. "Carefully stretch it back and she should be able to pass the baby."

I felt all around the mass my hand came into contact with, and Coco began pushing hard.

"I can't find the back legs and she is pushing."

"Wait a minute."

He must have placed his phone on the ground and I could hear him and Penelope grunting.

"Are you okay?" I shouted.

"Yes, yes. Baby is out. Keep trying to get the back leg out. I'll be down in five minutes."

I kept trying but with no luck. The five minutes seemed like an hour. At last Antonio appeared at the stable door.

"You have delivered breech births before. What's the problem this time?"

He had had a long day and night so I couldn't blame him for being grumpy.

"I can't find the back leg. I really can't."

Antonio closed his eyes and went in. Coco cried and pushed.

"It's a bad one, Diane."

He tried to manoeuvre the baby's back leg.

"You have to put your thumb on the kid's bum

Jonathan

and push it back in. That will give me room to move the back leg."

Coco wanted to lie down.

"Don't let her go down, Pedro. She will push even harder."

Coco cried louder. I knew we could lose the babies because it was taking too long to get this first baby out. I pushed the baby further back inside and Antonio, concentrating hard, visualised where the hind leg was. Steadily, he pulled it back, pushed my hand out of the way, and delivered a huge boy. I cleared his airways and, thank heavens, he cried. I placed him in front of Coco and she happily cleaned him.

"Quickly, bump her tummy," Antonio said.

I lifted her tummy, which brought the other baby into the birth canal, and Antonio delivered a little girl.

"Swing her," he instructed, as he stood up and bumped Coco's tummy again.

I cleaned the little girl's mouth and gently swung her to drain all the mucus from her airways. She, too, cried. I handed her over to her mum. Antonio delivered a third larger boy. He was fine. A quick rub and that wonderful sound rang out: *Waaaaaa!*

Antonio rolled a cigarette and waited to make sure all the afterbirth had come away.

"Hot chocolate?" I asked.

"Yes, please," both men chorused.

By the time I returned with biscuits and mugs of hot chocolate, Antonio had latched all three onto Coco.

"I did say it was tricky," I said to Antonio.

"Tricky, yes. Impossible, no. Always remain calm, Diane, and work the problem."

"I know, I know. But it's Coco," I said quietly.

"Diane, it was a difficult birth. It was difficult for me but you have to keep going. You must focus and find a way."

He was right. Coco had the same problem a year later and I delivered all three. But I decided it was time to retire her. One day I may not be there at the right time and she could die.

Now Coco is having a different kind of problem. One evening, bringing the goats back from the hills, Coco wasn't with them. Darkness fell and we searched for her with our torches but with no luck. I made my usual panic call.

"Antonio, Coco is missing on the hill. We can't find her."

"She will come down in the morning, Diane. Instinct will keep her high and in a bush. Trust me."

I hardly slept, thinking about my sweet Coco alone, scared, and on a hill. I had failed to keep her safe. Wild dogs might attack her or she could be trapped in a snare. Aliens might abduct her. At first light, I was outside, and there she was, waiting by the gate, ready to come in and eat breakfast.

From that day onward, Mikki took over as Coco's guardian. Mikki had made incredible progress since the day Antonio carried her down to us when she was three months old. Pete had helped her walk and slowly built up her muscle strength. She had become a mother and produced a high quantity of milk. Peter calls her his Angel and Mikki is the guardian Angel of all the goats that have problems. She understood how vulnerable a disability made them within the herd. She also understood that a goat needs to know its limitations.

Gerona was one goat who found it really hard to accept her disability. Her leg had been very badly broken in an accident. Bones had become infected and it was a mess. I persevered with treatment and the outcome, although not perfect, enabled her to walk out with the goats, climb hills, have babies and be milked. Three of her legs were strong and her bent leg balanced her in an odd way. But it worked.

As she got older, hill climbing tired her. But she wouldn't give up and walk on the lower, easier, path with Mikki, Coco and Ruby. She persevered but Mikki and I noticed she was resting more. My efforts to persuade Gerona to stay with us old gals landed on very deaf ears.

Gerona would not listen to the human idiot and so Mikki stepped in.

One afternoon the goats took off, climbing high on a hill. It was a muggy afternoon with lots of flies and other biting insects zooming around our heads. Rita and I led the special needs, plus the sheep, on the lower path and I sighed as Gerona, yet again, began to make the climb. Mikki shot off after her and Gerona stopped climbing. I continued walking as this was goat business. Ten minutes later Mikki appeared with Gerona walking behind her. From that day forward Gerona always took the easy route, with no loss of dignity.

Coco's time for walking out with the herd was slowly coming to an end. I wanted to keep her safely at home, but this stressed her, and so out she came.

Mikki stepped up her protection. She stood next to her when she ate and gently guided her back to the farm, keeping her away from the rest of the herd and protecting her from being bumped and pushed.

Mikki lay close to Coco the night she passed away.

Jonathan

The most rewarding thing on the farm was watching the animals' characters develop. The ones with disabilities seemed to balance their special needs with huge personalities.

Katy, with her cleft palate, was demanding but full of fun. Lulu waved her disabled paw around in a majestic manner to all who walked by. She, too, was demanding. She insisted on having the best dog beds, two sun loungers, inside and outside. She loved little Martin but insisted he kept the pesky Katy away from her.

"Katy needs a job," said Pete, after serenading her to sleep.

"For goodness sake what sort of job, other than amusing us with her dance moves? I think she is the family Joker."

"Yes, she is the Jester on the farm, but we have to find a proper job for her."

I realised he had drunk two beers on an empty stomach. A pie was in the oven and would be ready in fifteen minutes. Pete reached for a third can which was unusual. I raised my eyebrow Roger Moore style.

"I'm having another beer!"

"Okay, that's fine," I said hastily because I sensed one of those pointless bickering sessions coming on that we both could do without.

"I'm worried about the car, the well pump, the generator needing a service and we are broke."

He fiddled with the third beer but hadn't taken a sip.

"I know, I know. And we still have five goats due to give birth. Cheers!" I clinked my half glass of wine against his small can of beer.

The following day, Katy had found employment.

We kept the girls local, since five were due to give birth at any hour of any day. Sandra and Vinni had 'bagged up', an expression we used for udders filling up. It was also a sign of an impending birth. I thought it wise to come in half an hour earlier. The goats pottered through to the paddock by the house to eat hay before their main course was served.

Pete and I wanted the pregnant mums to be fed in their birthing pens. Katy was standing on the other side of the fence talking to the goats as they walked by.

"What is she doing?" Peter wanted to know.

"Hang on, I'll ask her." I turned to Katy. "What are you saying to the girls Katy?"

Rita Mae sat next to Katy to help explain to me Katy's new employment.

"Okay, 'Ealth and Safety Officer is me new job," Katy said in her broad Lancashire accent.

I immediately turned to Rita Mae.

"Did she say Health and Safety Officer?"

Jonathan

"I believe so," Rita confirmed in her soft sing-song voice.

"But what is she asking them?"

"I believe," answered Rita, who is an expert in practically everything, "I believe she is asking if they have any complaints against you or us dogs."

I am speechless but feel I should let her continue as it is giving Monty a rest from having to play football after a long day.

I relayed the conversation to my husband.

"If it keeps her happy," was Pete's opinion. "Trouble is, if there is a complaint and Rita Mae takes on the case, we could all be in trouble."

I stared at Pete then quickly recognised a case of *campo* madness. Hunger and an impending late night helping to birth baby goats, had got to him.

"I'll get some dinner on. Sausage, egg and chips will be quick. How does that sound?"

"Perfect, I'll finish up here. Perhaps Katy could ask ME about 'Ealth and Safety. That will keep her occupied for the rest of the night."

My husband's sarcastic remarks, aimed at a tiny special needs goat, clearly showed me that I needed to pour him a shot glass of brandy and place it on the table before he tucked into his dinner.

We didn't bother to change out of our work clothes before eating. As the last bit of egg was mopped up with bread, we took a moment to enjoy the feeling of fullness. Then boots were pulled on and we went back to the stable. Sandra started to push as soon as she saw us.

"Game on," I said.

Sandra birthed two big boys and I latched them onto the milk bar. Vinnie was up next. We hoped for one big kid since Vinnie only had one working teat. The other was damaged in an accident she had in Salado two years before. Our hopes were dashed when Pete delivered two big babies, a boy and a girl.

"Okay, Pete, let the boy have some colostrum now, then he goes into the crèche."

I hoped I had enough colostrum stored in the freezer to feed him for a few more days. Plus enough for any other kids that may have to go into the crèche.

By 1 am Welfi had given birth to two boys. I made the decision to put the largest boy into the crèche. Welfi had not produced enough milk. Another hour was spent warming up the stored colostrum and feeding the babies until they were full and sleepy. I dipped all their umbilical cords in iodine and checked Alma and Louise. They were no further along. At 2:30 am we climbed into bed. Three hours later the alarm went off.

"No, no, no," moaned Peter.

"Yes, yes, yes," I moaned back.

We slowly turned to meet each other's eyes. It

took a few moments before we both realised we were awake and the alarm was screaming.

The dogs woke up and Katy banged on the wall from House Two, demanding breakfast. The horses were already banging on the back gate waiting for their early morning buckets. We then had the same conversation that we have every morning.

"They can bloody well wait for their feed. I want a cup of tea," said Peter, pulling on his boots.

"Absolutely. We have tea and biscuits before we do anything." I zipped up my fleece.

With Katy, dogs and horses fed, we finally sat with a mug of tea and dippy rich tea biscuits. The colostrum was slowly warming on the stove. Then revved up, and with the colostrum poured into bottles, we shuffled into the goat shed to be met with mayhem. New mothers and their babies, and all the kids that were in the crèche, were out and had mixed with the rest of the herd.

"Oh, no, no, no!" Pete cried.

New mums were calling for their babies. Goats were head-butting babies who were searching for their mothers, asking every goat they bumped into, "Are you my mummy?"

The birthing pens had been wrecked. No time to figure out how it happened. We had to sort out this mess.

"Pete, put the mums in the milking shed."

While Pete dragged the new mums into the other stable, I gathered up the new babies. I realised Alma and Louise had given birth in the night but had no idea which baby belonged to which mum. Finally, all the kids were gathered and placed on one side of the stable. I couldn't remember who belonged to whom. Peter was just as confused. Also, with the new kids of Alma and Louise thrown in the mix, this could get messy.

Vinnie's little girl bounced up to her mother, but the boys looked confused. Half an hour later we re-united mums and offspring but we had one left over. Two were in the crèche last night so who did this one belong to? It must have been Alma. She had rejected one of her boys. It mattered not. I gave bottles to the babies, checked that the others were drinking well from their mothers while Pete reconstructed the pens.

Two hours later we staggered out of the sheds to be met with Katy demanding her walk and the dogs looking at me with pleading eyes. They do not like using the yard as a toilet.

"Who's idea was this goat malarkey?" said Pete.

"Yours, Peter!"

Nearly a week later we noticed that one of the boys had an enlarged knee and was in trouble. I immediately put him on a course of antibiotics but it didn't improve.

Pete formed a close bond with the little palomino-coloured boy. He bottle-fed him and carried him around, only putting him down when he needed both hands to do a job.

"We have to cure him, Diane."

"Pete, there is no cure. I can only think he must have got his umbilical cord infected the night the kids escaped. His problem is serious."

"We cured Mikki," he said, and I noted a tone of desperation in his voice.

"We didn't cure Mikki, Pete, we helped her walk. This boy is in pain. His joints are hurting him."

My brain was searching every cell to come up with a solution.

"He is staying with us and I have to find a name for him," said Peter.

"Okay. You wanted to call a boy Lemmy, didn't you?"

Yes, or Dave or Trigger. I'll have a think." He walked back into the goat shed.

An hour later he was back in the house with the kid cradled in his arms.

"So, what name did you decide on? I bet it's Lemmy."

Jonathan

"I thought I would call him Trigger but he told me his name," he said, smiling down at the little boy.

"He told you his name?"

"Yes, he told me his name is Jonathan."

Drama in Salado

Antonio has steadily been getting stronger over the months. He is still taking medication, making his face look puffy, but, all in all, his health has been improving. We met up at the Lost Garden while he waited for Agustin to bring the goats home. A few weeks earlier, Pete had helped him move the equipment and goats to his summer residence, the Molino.

Today he phones me from his home in Olvera, asking for help with a buck.

"What buck?"

"I am borrowing the black buck from Chari's aunt down the road. It's a pure Muciano. I need to begin a new breeding programme."

Muciano is a much sought-after breed.

"Okay, we will be at your place at midday."

Two hours later we arrive at Antonio's house to find him impatiently revving his Land Rover, his wife talking loudly to him through the window.

"He is not supposed to be handling a buck," Chari says to me, her voice still a tad loud.

"We are here to help," I say, smiling my best smile.

I jump out of our car as Chari walks back into the house, muttering under her breath.

"What are we doing?" I ask through his open window.

"We are picking up Fernando. I may need help lifting him into the Land Rover."

"Okay, lead the way."

We follow his Land Rover down a track close to his house and there is Chari's aunt, waiting for us.

"He is in here," she says, and points at a large dog pen.

He backs the Land Rover as close as he can to the pen with Peter guiding him.

Antonio should have no problem handling a buck, but I assume Chari has instructed everyone that her husband must not overdo it.

"Plan?" I ask him.

"Pedro you hold his back leg. Diane and I will lift his front legs into the Land Rover."

The handsome black boy is as quiet as a lamb.

Drama in Salado

He only kicks Peter twice before we manoeuvre him into the back of the truck.

"Thank you," says Antonio, as he jumps into the Land Rover and starts the engine.

He revs the truck a few times. I get the message.

"Antonio, shall we come down to the mill and help you get him out of the truck?"

"No, no. I can manage," he says, still revving.

I turn to Pete. "Follow us to his father's track. We are going to the mill."

I jump into the Land Rover and Antonio immediately pulls away. We drive in silence until we reach the track leading down to the mill. We pull up and Pete joins us. We bounce down the track to the mill.

Antonio brakes hard as we arrive. Goat and humans lurch forward. Fernando's eyes are wide and he looks terrified.

"Where are we putting him?"

"Agustin and I have made a special paddock for him and a few goats."

We inspect the paddock. Fernando is rocking the Land Rover.

"I think we should get the boy out, Antonio, before he wrecks your truck."

Antonio grabs a rope from inside the mill. Peter is standing by the Land Rover's back door wondering which leg of the wide-eyed, frightened buck he should grab. I am not sure how strong Antonio is and I don't want to embarrass this proud man by taking over.

"Okay, Pedro, open the back door," he tells my husband.

Peter is searching my eyes looking for instructions. Finding none, he opens the back door. Antonio slips the rope over the buck's neck and walks forward. Fernando meekly follows. Pete and I walk stooped over, ready to grab one of Fernando's back legs should he become unruly. Either the goat was still in shock or Antonio was using goat whispering to keep him calm. After turning him loose to meet his new girlfriends, Antonio sits down on a wall to catch his breath.

"So, no Salado this year?"

"No Salado, Diane. I'm close to home and it's easier for Agustin. And Bernado can come to work too."

I look at my friend. I know the medication has altered his face, making it puffy, but there is something else. I think he is scared. I think something in his personality has changed. I can't explain what, but there is something different.

"Chari is helping too," he says suddenly. "But she cleans, that's all. She doesn't understand animals."

"She is helping and that's all that matters."

"Animals tell you everything," he says quietly.

Drama in Salado

I decide not to question him any further as he is again staring vacantly into the distance.

"Time for a lift back up the track," I say, smiling, and this snaps him back to earth.

"Have you much milk to sell?" he asks, as he races up the bumpy track, not sparing our bones.

Pete and I exchange glances.

"No, not much, just enough for ourselves. The girls are mostly dry now. I'm glad you are here this summer and not in Salado. Too much drama over there."

"Yes, Diane, too much drama, and I've had enough this year."

Pete starts up our car while I watch Antonio drive back to the mill.

"He looks so much better, don't you think?"

I smile and nod. Deep down I know something is off. The old Antonio needs to rest a bit longer. Time will tell.

The good news is, he is not taking the goats to Salado. Too much drama.

Antonio was not offended when I declined to take my girls to Salado for the summer. I liked to think he understood that my goats preferred to sleep in their own beds at night. They were comfortable in the familiarity of Las Vicarias.

I liked to think he understood that it also gave me more time to prepare meals, hang out washing and have time to sit for an hour in the evenings, listening to music, before bedtime.

I liked to think that but I knew it was a lie. He thought I pampered my girls. He thought I was depriving them of good food that the land in Salado offered. He had no comprehension of domestic duties and music didn't move him. Except Bruce Springsteen. But, of course, he didn't understand the lyrics.

In fact, the upside of me not having my goats in Salado was the lack of argument between us. However, it didn't stop him from asking me to drive over with medicine, trimmers, or to help with worming, blood testing, and any other thing that needed a second pair of hands. He was always happy to see me but I'm sure he sighed with relief when I left and the bickering stopped.

I had been summoned to help worm his herd. Pete and I, luckily, had collected a huge amount of olive cuttings for our herd and so I was free to leave the farm. On arrival, I was met with Antonio battling to worm the goats on his own. I stood and watched the chaos as the control gate of his worming-pen was being crashed into by the waiting goats. Antonio swore loudly until he realised I was watching.

"Why didn't you wait for me?" I said, hands

Drama in Salado

on hips. I enjoyed seeing him lose his control. My smirk did not impress him.

"If I wait for you I could lose an hour."

"I'm on time," I said, pointing at my watch.

"Well, come and get working then, Diane. Don't just stand there."

And so the tone was set and the arguing began. He grabbed a goat and I drenched it with the wormer. He worked at an impossible pace. Goats were presented to me before I had drawn the next dose of wormer in the large syringe. Sweat was dripping off my chin and wasps were circling.

We were nearly finished, with only two goats left to be caught and brought to the pen. I spied two babies in the corner, one fast asleep and the other leaping around a stack of pallets. Antonio used these to make emergency pens.

"Who do these two babies belong to?"

"They are Nuria's. She is fed up with them."

"That white one will hurt itself on those pallets if she keeps jumping on them like that."

"Stop fussing and help push this goat."

He grappled with a girl who had put the brakes on and refused to enter the worming-pen.

I squirted the last of the medicine into the goat's mouth, narrowly avoiding one of her horns poking out my eye. I heard a cry.

"Told you," I said, running to the white kid.

Nuria, the mother, ran over to her baby as I examined the kid's front leg. I couldn't feel any broken bones and decided that she must have just wrenched it. I latched her on her mum for a comfort drink.

"She is beautiful. A little princess," I told Antonio

"Okay. We will call her Princessa."

Over the next few weeks, I visited Princessa, checking that her leg was improving. I carried her over to her rather useless mother, who had lost interest in her lame, baby girl.

"She is getting better," I said.

"No, she is not, Diane. I can't keep her and that's that. All the babies are off tomorrow."

"You can't. Princessa is beautiful."

"Stop, Diane, just stop. Not every story has a happy ending."

I pleaded for another hour, cuddled Princessa, but finally realised that I couldn't interfere with his herd. I left Salado crying.

Two days later I visited Antonio. Pete thought we should agree to a truce. I took a couple of cans of no-alcohol beer with me as a peace offering. He saw me approaching and pulled up two beer crates he used as chairs.

"Hello," he said, beaming.

"Hello," I said, matching his beam. "I bring beer."

Drama in Salado

We opened the cans and he began to tell me how well Cheeta was progressing as a guardian dog.

"She is so much like her father," he said proudly.

"Of course. Monty is the best."

"Look at her," he said, pointing to the corral. "She just lies with the goats and they love her."

I didn't want to look, I didn't want to see the empty corner that Princessa had lain in.

"Look, look," Antonio urged.

I slowly turned and there she was. Princessa in her usual place.

I rushed into the corral and cuddled her.

"What changed your mind?"

"I couldn't stand you shouting at me for the next year."

Over the following years, every time I visited Antonio, and Princess was being milked, I would say, "What words are you looking for, Antonio?"

"*Gracias*, Diane."

"*Gracias*, for what?"

"*Gracias* for Princessa."

The little white baby recovered from her injury and became his top milk producer, a brilliant mother, and one of his most loving goats.

Antonio phoned at least once a day when he was in Salado. He phoned just for a chat or to update me on dogs and certain goats. This was unusual for him. When he was home, either in the top sheds or in the Molino, he phoned to bark orders at me. Pete and I came to the conclusion that Antonio thinks of Salado as a different province, even though the area lies close to the town.

"The river is different, the land is different, it's not as friendly as Las Vicarias," he complained in one phone call.

"Well, why don't you just come back? We can help you move."

"Don't be ridiculous. There is good food here."

"Okay. Speak tomorrow."

I ended the call, shaking my head. The Spanish way of thinking is still a mystery to me.

One hot evening, Pete and I were enjoying watching Katy tap dance around the yard. It was too hot to put her to bed and far too sticky for us to try and sleep. As I poured cold beer into our glasses, the phone rang.

"Hello, Antonio," I said, staring at the cold beer waiting to be sipped.

"I can't find Joanna and Cheeta isn't here."

"Oh no! Do you want us to come over to help you find them?" I looked at Pete.

Drama in Salado

My husband put his beer down and let out a loud sigh.

"No. Joanna will be okay if Cheeta is with her."

Now I was puzzled. Joanna is a sweet young baby. She had been weaned and was finding her way within the herd. Cheeta was still a young dog. Would she know that she should stay close and protect the little goat?

"Are you sure they are both together, Antonio?"

"They must be. It's too dark to go looking for them now. I'll take the goats on the same route in the morning to look for them. Have a good night. Bye."

"Why did he phone, Pete?"

"Diane, he was just thinking it through that's all. And the heat may have got to him."

We finished the beers and Pete sang to Katy to prepare her for bed. I sent a prayer up for the two missing animals and Monty put his head on my lap.

"Mummy, my daughter will know what to do. She is of royal blood," he reassured me.

"If Antonio can't find her, you must come with me to help search for them," I told him, my head resting on his.

The following morning, at 9:30 am, Antonio called.

"Found them," he said.

"Where? What happened? Are they okay?"

"I walked the goats for about an hour on the track by the river and suddenly Cheeta appeared from behind a bush, with Joanna following her. Cheeta stayed with her to keep her safe. What a dog, Diane, what a dog."

I rushed into the sheds and told Pete, then found Monty and told him how wonderful his daughter was.

"Mummy, it is her duty. I would expect nothing less from her," his eyes told me.

Monty was right, and three weeks later Cheeta would prove herself to be the great guardian dog that she was born to be.

˜˜˜

August *Feria* had come and gone. Antonio was watching the skies for any threat of a storm and we were doing the same at Las Vicarias. This time of year could be very dangerous. Flash floods only gave us minutes to get clear of the river. The corrals in Salado were right next to the river. Antonio was already talking about coming back to Las Vicarias and Pete was waiting for the phone call to come and help him move back home.

After a warm evening watching Katy play, dusk was approaching so Pete reached for his guitar to calm the little goat down, ready for bed. My phone rang.

"Hello, is it time to come back to Las Vicarias, Antonio?"

"Miracle has fallen down a well," he said, panic in his voice.

"What? Wait. You say little Miracle has fallen in a well? What bloody well?"

"I'm downriver just off the track. The lid is off. I can see her but I don't know what she is standing on or if there is water under her and she is sinking. It was Cheeta who found her."

"Start from the beginning," I said trying to calm him down.

"No time. Oh God, look. Cheeta came to the corral, barked and barked then ran away. She kept doing that until I followed her and here I am. I don't know how I'm going to get her out."

It was nearly dark and we needed a plan.

"Antonio, is there a ladder in your brother's sheds?"

"I'll go and look and I'll phone you back."

This was something new. It is always us who phoned El Maestro when things went wrong. Maybe it was being at Salado that got him spooked.

The phone rang, and I picked up before the second buzz.

"No ladder and everything is locked up. Miracle is panicking."

While talking to me he was also trying to reassure the little goat.

I had now worked out the problem. Antonio hates closed spaces and water. A deep well epitomised all those horrors. And an animal in distress would only increase his anxiety.

"Antonio, I have a plan. Drive the Land Rover to the well, attach your tow rope and then you have to climb down to get Miracle."

"Okay, but I have to climb back up with a goat and I don't know if the bottom is full of mud. I could sink."

"Just get the bloody Land Rover, Antonio, and I'll think some more."

The phone went dead. Five minutes later it rang again.

"Antonio, I think—"

He cut me off.

"It's okay, I can sort it, I'll put the phone on the ground so if I have an accident you can call Nacho for help."

I smiled. El Maestro was back in control.

Pete and I put my phone on speaker and we leant forward to catch every sound.

Everything was muffled but at least we couldn't hear a splash, so that was a good sign. About ten minutes later he picked up the phone.

"Got her. I've put her in the truck. I need to get her back to the herd and give Cheeta double rations. I'll explain tomorrow."

The following morning, while we were eating toast and sipping tea, Antonio phoned.

"There wasn't much room but I climbed down. I didn't put my feet on the bottom in case mud sucked my boots off. I grabbed Miracle by her front leg, swung her round my neck, then climbed back up the rope very fast before she fell off."

"Wow, Antonio, that was some rescue!"

"It was Cheeta who saved her. She didn't leave the side of the well until I lifted her out," he said quietly. "Can Pedro help tomorrow to move us back home?"

"Of course he can. Las Vicarias is missing you."

A shock and a battle

It's nearly the end of January. One month into 2016 and it's the last month of birthing for Antonio. Walking into Antonio's sheds to deliver vitamins, I decide not to tell him that Pete and I will be retiring the goats this year. Agustin greets me, grinning.

"Hello, Diane."

"Hello, Agustin. Where is Antonio?"

"At the back, checking babies."

I find Antonio lifting up and examining a kid.

"Are you okay?" I ask.

"Yes. Just making sure the kids are drinking properly."

His eyes don't meet mine. I can hear a slight change in his speech. Not much but he doesn't sound quite right.

"Speak," I tell him.

"What!"

"Say something. You don't sound right."

"I'm fine. My back hurts, that's all."

He looks up and I can see the pain in his eyes.

"Antonio, you must go back to Malaga. Your back hurting was the start of your troubles last year."

"Don't be ridiculous. There is nothing wrong. I have tablets. Feeding babies will make anyone's back hurt."

I look at him and realise that I won't be able to get his alarm bells ringing. His face has the moon shape of a person on steroids. His left eye looks a bit droopy. Why hasn't anyone else noticed?

This year, Chari and Agustin are working with Antonio. Pete and I have stepped away, only helping in a birthing emergency. We need to catch up on a year's work and plan for the coming years.

I walk down the narrow path back to our farm. I have a full view of the damage the winter has done to our land. Our banks have been washed away and the river has cut a gorge through our land. We cannot afford to fix the banks and so we hope the last months of winter will be gentle with us.

I enter the goat sheds to check if everyone is doing well. We are steadily drying the girls off. Fewer births means less milk. We currently have

A shock and a battle

enough milk to make rice puddings and quiches. The dogs and cats will drink any surplus.

New European Union regulations, for small farmers, have made it impossible for us to carry on and we are relieved. The price of animal feed has increased so much that we cannot break even at the end of the month.

And our hearts ache too much when we have to sell the babies. Pete and I are not cut out to be farmers. We have to find another source of income. We cannot sell our girls. They have provided us with an income for many years and they deserve a nice retirement.

I pop into Chinni's special stable that she shares with Ruby. Both goats are unable to walk out with the herd. They have their own paddock, a stable, and extra-special care. A visiting vet could not believe how Chinni has survived with her multiple problems. He could not grasp Chinni's will to live. Sitting with her always puts my problems and worries into perspective. She gives me strength to overcome life's hurdles. She allows me to give her a hug and I go into the house to prepare lunch.

I leave my phone on the outside table because my friend, Eileen, is due back from the UK any time now. We have the same routine. Eileen briskly leaves Arrivals and phones her husband, Frank, who is parked five minutes away. She then lights up a cigarette and phones me. The conversation is always the same.

"You better not have broken anything while I've been away," she will say.

This is followed by a list of 'bits' she has brought back for me. She insists I have Kendal Mint Cake in the winter and multi-vitamins in the summer. She never forgets her friend.

The vegetable stew is bubbling away and it's time to plonk the dumplings in. The phone chirps.

"I'm coming, Eileen, one second," I shout at the phone.

I wipe flour off my hands, onto my jeans, and grab the phone from the table.

"Welcome home, Eileen!"

"It's Frank, Diane. Are you sitting down?"

"Hang on, I'll pull up a chair."

I am excited as this call could mean that Eileen has at last won the Euro Millions and our problems are over.

"I'm here, Frank, where's Eileen?"

"She is dead, Diane. She died on the plane."

"Eileen dead? No, no, wait. PETE! Frank, tell Pete."

"What's happened?" Pete asks me.

"Take the phone," I say, and hand it over to him.

I watch Pete's face, hoping I have misheard. He paces round and round, listening to Eileen's

A shock and a battle

husband. Pete interjects with, "Yes, I understand. I'll make the call. Alright, Frank."

Finally, the call ends, and my husband turns to look into my eyes.

"She has gone, Diane. She died on the plane. Anne Marie is going to help Frank with the police. Eileen has gone."

Peter reaches out to me but I am beyond comfort. Eileen Hair, wife, mother, grandmother, friend, has left us.

I want to run, scream, punch walls. Anything to express my pain. I do all three while Pete looks on, helpless. I walk past the dogs and my husband to enter Chinni's stable.

I know her calm energy will focus me. It will show us how we can all go forward in life, without Eileen.

Time passes and I get up from the stable floor. The winter sun hits my eyes and it begins to dry the tears on my face. Peter is waiting and hands me a mug of coffee.

"I've put brandy in it, Di," he says quietly.

"Thank you. I'll drink this and then we make the phone calls."

My husband knows me well. He knows how practical I am. He knows I am in survival mode. He knows that tonight, much later tonight, he will hold me while I cry myself to sleep, grieving for the loss of my friend, my Eileen, my Angel.

Little Jonathan had made friends with the two other bottle-fed babies. We named one after our friend, Eugene, and the other blond, pretty boy, I named Yum Yum. He was not named after Nanki Poo's love in the Mikado. He was named Yum Yum because that was the sound he made when he drank from his bottle.

Jonathan played as much as his leg allowed. I had finished the course of strong antibiotics and we were waiting to see if he had improved. He would often lie down to watch Eugene and Yummy play chase in the stable.

It saddened Pete that his boy couldn't join in the fun. He spent a lot of time sitting and chatting with him and even toyed with the idea of letting him join Katy. I promptly scuppered that idea.

"Katy will bully him. You know what she is like."

"I know but he seems so alone when the other two are running around and he can't."

A day later Jonathan had a new friend. Her name was Gracie.

A week before the boys were born, Lolly had given birth to a boy and girl. Within hours they became ill. I put them into a quarantine/hospice pen, administrating medicine that the cooperative vet had prescribed. I lost the boy and the pretty

A shock and a battle

white girl was fading. I decided to stop the vet's medicine and, for two days, gave her bicarb of soda and no milk. It was a case of kill or cure. Placing her in a cat travel box I said goodnight, holding no expectations of finding her alive in the morning.

Opening the stable door the next day, Gracie crawled out and was calling for food. Within a week she was up and running. I felt she was strong enough to join the boys. Gracie was immediately drawn to Jonathan. She seemed to understand he had a problem and became his best friend.

I asked Antonio to come and examine Jonathan. The last round of antibiotics had not helped at all.

"Should I take him to the vet, Antonio? I have run out of ideas."

"You want the truth, Diane?"

"Yes, I want the truth."

"He can't be cured. His joints are infected and eventually his brain will be infected. If you take him to the vet he will tell you it's over and put him to sleep."

"Maybe it's for the best."

"Are you crazy? Are you giving up?"

"Antonio, you told me there is no cure."

"There is no cure for Mikki, no cure for Katy but they are still here. Not to mention Gerona and Ruby."

"So what should I do?"

"Okay, didn't you tell me that there are two English vets that have a holiday home in Olvera?"

"Yes, Graham and Zoe."

"Take Jonathan to them and see if they have some English ideas."

At last, I had a plan and could do something positive. The following day I phoned Zoe and asked if I could bring a young goat to the house for her to examine, apologising for interrupting their holiday time."

"Yes, of course," she said. "I love goats. Can't wait to meet him."

Thankfully I always have a stack of nappies (diapers) in my medicine cabinet. They have multiple uses, especially if an animal has an injury. Tomorrow will be the first time they will be put to their proper use.

Peter placed Jonathan, wearing a nappy, on my lap and we shared the seat belt. He seemed to love the car journey and enjoyed the fuss people made of him after we parked the car and walked up the narrow street to our friends' house.

"Ah, I see the problem," said Graham, opening the door. "The goat is here, Zoe. Come and have a look."

Zoe appeared with a beaming smile.

"Oh, he is beautiful," she said, stroking Jonathan's head.

A shock and a battle

She carefully inspected his knee.

"I'll put the kettle on," she said.

Graham took over and gave him a thorough examination. He waited until Zoe returned with coffee before revealing his thoughts.

"Diane, he can't fully recover from this."

My face dropped.

"He won't recover. But we can give him a chance at life. Put him on another course of antibiotics but this time, hit it harder. Ten-day course plus vitamins. Splint his good leg. It is taking too much weight and it will buckle. If there is no improvement, or if his knee gets bigger, or his pain increases, he has to be put down. Give him six weeks."

"Okay, I can do that. But he will be a pin cushion by the end of ten days."

Zoe saw my pain and worry. She led me into the kitchen and told me to put Jonathan down on the tiles. Graham led Pete upstairs to see his (Graham's) latest renovation project.

"Diane, goats are strong. Look at him, he wants to live. After ten days, if there's no improvement, give him a two-week break and then hit it again. It will be okay."

Graham and Zoe had given us hope and a plan of action. As soon as we arrived home, Pete began customising a splint for Jonathan's good leg. I took his nappy off and he hopped away with his friend, Gracie, to tell her of his adventures in the big world. She had been waiting for her chum by the stable door.

The following day we drove into town to collect a new batch of antibiotics and a bunch of syringes. We were trying to work out how we were going to pay for the medicine.

"I'm turning into a rabbit, eating bloody lettuce sandwiches," Peter said. "We need food, proper food."

"We need money," I said. "We need a miracle to happen today. I am running out of ideas. We could buy sardines. We have potatoes so that should fill us up."

Pete gave me a look I couldn't decipher. His phone rang and I answered it.

"Hello, love," said a familiar voice. " Is Pete there?"

"Yes, Anne Marie, but he is driving. What's up?"

"Wondering if he is free this week to do some painting in a house we are selling?"

Anne Marie is an estate agent and our friend. Zoe and Anne Marie, of Olvera Properties, often give Pete odd jobs to do. It helps them and boosts our income.

"Yes, yes, and yes please!" I said, bouncing on my seat. "We are nearly in town. Meet you for coffee?"

A shock and a battle

We arrived back at the farm with a bag of food, a big bottle of antibiotics, and the knowledge that we had more money coming in at the end of the week.

Pete dashed into the stables to check on Jonathan while I sorted out the medicine. For the first time in days, I began to hum. The dogs sensed my mood had changed and their tails wagged.

"Diane, he has more problems," said Peter, coming in from the sheds.

He lent on the kitchen table with a look of despair. The atmosphere changed and the dogs returned to their beds.

"What now?"

"Come and look," he said.

I followed Pete back to the stable to see Jonathan standing on three legs, looking very distressed.

"Look at his knee," said Peter, picking up the little boy.

Gently, I felt around his swollen knee and Jonathan cried out.

"Ok, quickly feed the goats hay. I need to think."

"It's pus, isn't it?" Peter asked.

"Yes, it's pus and I have to get it out."

After researching every farm and vet on the Internet, I discovered how to draw out the pus quickly and carefully. Luckily, I had a spray that temporarily numbs an injected site. It was all systems go. I had to hold my nerve and take the pain away from the little boy. I reminded myself that I had performed many procedures on goats and I could do this one.

Half an hour later, I had all the pus out, antibiotics administered, the leg bandaged, and a happier, pain-free goat. Gingerly, he put his bad leg down on the ground. We breathed sighs of relief when Gracie bounced up to him and, together, they walked away into their little paddock.

I knew I couldn't celebrate yet because the infection could return. For the next ten days, Jonathan buried his head into Pete while I injected him. Twice more, I cleared pus out, and at the end of the ten-day course, he could run and play. He still had a slight limp, but nothing that would hold him back from living his best life.

17

Roger

Agustin phones me.

"Antonio is in hospital."

"Why, when?"

"Two nights ago."

"Why didn't you tell me before? What's happened?"

"I think he had a fever and was not right in his head," is his vague response.

"Okay. Well, keep me updated," I say, knowing he won't.

"Peter, phone Nacho. Antonio is in hospital and Agustin doesn't really know what's happened."

Pete takes his phone out to the olive grove to get a better signal. I wait and pace.

"They are operating tomorrow," Pete says, walking back into the house. "Apparently it's to clean his brain."

"What does that mean? His brain isn't a bloody house that needs hoovering!" I almost laugh. Maybe hysterics is setting in.

"All Nacho said was that he has a fever and that he was sleeping again. When they got him to hospital, in Ronda, he was transferred to Malaga. Oh, and he needs another operation."

"He has an infection. It must be an infection. It must be bad if they are operating."

"We just have to wait and see, Diane. Nacho will phone me with any more news."

Antonio's goats are at the Molino, which is easier for Agustin. He can drive Antonio's Land Rover off-road to get there. His herd is pregnant so only a few goats need milking.

"I knew he wasn't right. Let's hope this time he can be properly fixed."

I wait for Peter to tell me everything is going to be fine and that Antonio will be back soon. He doesn't.

"Diane, I think Antonio is in big trouble. I think the family knows it and they are not telling us. Or Antonio for that matter. I hope I am wrong."

I look at Pete. I trust his gut feelings. He is

rarely wrong. I walk outside and look up at the skies. Clear and blue with the sun blazing down.

But now I feel a heaviness is enveloping Las Vicarias.

※ ※ ※

Bailey and Hardy have bonded and are enjoying retirement. They potter around the valley during the night, come in for breakfast, and then potter some more until midday when it's too hot to be outside. Lunch is served at 12:30 pm, tea at 5:30 pm. Then they walk around the valley to eat and sleep.

Occasionally, they slip under the electric tape, which we string across the river, to prevent them from going either up or downriver. Our neighbour has sown his largest pasture with barley and oats. The boys saw a green field and wanted to get to it. Pete strengthened the fence.

It was breakfast time. I got up early, trying to get ahead before the day chucked the usual surprises at us. I made up the horses' breakfast, then walked out into the goats' paddock to check everyone was okay and no family disputes had occurred overnight. Hardy was standing by the fence pawing the ground.

"Okay, okay, Hardy. Breakfast is coming up. Where is Bailey?"

Hardy snorted and I saw Bailey behind him, lying flat out. He was not asleep.

"PETER!" I screamed and ran round to the horses' gate, my heart racing.

"What's the matter?" Peter called, trying to catch up with me.

"It's Bailey. He's down."

I ran to the old boy's side. His mouth was wide open, his eyes bulging.

"Pete, phone the vet. It's colic and he is bad."

He ran to the olive grove to get a strong signal.

"She's coming," Pete said, and I noticed his hand was shaking.

This was the second time he had seen a horse with colic. We lost our beautiful boy, Beau, a few years before and now our rescue horse was lying down and in great pain.

"Peter, go and get Hardy's breakfast and feed him in the stable. I'm going to get Bailey on his feet."

I lifted Bailey's head, clipped his head collar on, positioned his legs and got him up. I gently walked him in circles. Every minute that passed seemed an eternity. Our horse vet came racing down the track and I could now hand over responsibility.

Marina examined Bailey, gave him a jab and then we had to tube him to clear his gut. The old boy, who hates being fussed over, was a perfect patient. He was in pain but seemed to know we were helping him. Two hours later our wonderful vet had done as much as she could, which included acupuncture.

"Diane, he needs to gently walk now until he poos and his stomach is working properly. It may be a long night for you. Call me in the morning and give me an update."

I hugged her and felt very alone when she drove away. Now it was up to me to get Bailey through this.

Pete and I took turns walking him. By nightfall, Hardy was fed up and kept getting in the way by pulling at the lead rope. I made the decision to unclip Bailey, hoping he would continue to follow me without Hardy's interference.

It worked. It was a perfect join-up. I weaved around the olive trees with Bailey tight on my shoulder. Peter brought out my head torch and then gave me an update on the animals. He assured me that giving the goats the last bales of hay was necessary.

"Has he had a poo?" Pete wanted to know.

"No, nothing yet, but I've got an idea, Keep your fingers crossed. I hope it works."

I walked up the steep piece of land behind the house, which meant that Bailey had to push himself to follow me. I did this twice and I then I heard the best sound, pure music to my ears. Bailey farted long and loud.

"YES!" I shouted, stroking his neck. "Now you have to poo."

As I walked him towards the river, he raised his tail to poo, before farting some more. Hardy was waiting for him on the river bank. I let them walk around the river for an hour, while I had the sandwich that would soak up the glass of wine I desperately needed. My plan was to bring the boys back into the secure paddock so I could check on Bailey through the night. While I gulped my wine, Pete may have solved the problem of how Bailey got colic.

"He lifted the electric fence with his head and walked into the neighbour's field."

"But what about Hardy?"

"He is too tall to get under. I'll double up the fence first thing in the morning."

I refilled my glass but, this time, sipped slowly. Peter refilled his beer and we clinked glasses.

"To loud farts," said Peter.

"To loud farts," I echoed.

Before Paz crossed the rainbow bridge, somebody else came into our lives. We needed another stable. Pete built an extension on the original stable, but we needed more space to milk. We had saved and bought building blocks during the previous year. Other than cement and sand, we were ready to go.

"I need help, Diane, I can't do this by myself. It's too much."

"We can't afford to pay for help," I said, stating the blimmin' obvious.

What to do? The answer came the following day. A chance meeting with friends in the town solved our problem.

"You need a 'workaway'," suggested Rona, who was visiting from the next village.

"What's a 'workaway'?"

"A person comes to help for a specific time. All you do is feed them and they give you around five hours work a day."

I immediately got on to the 'workaway' website to look for a young man who was willing to build in the Andalusian heat. Many profiles came up but none, I felt, suited us. My youngest daughter phoned and I explained my dilemma.

"The trouble with you, Mother," Fliss said, in her usual blunt way, "is that you hate people staying with you."

"That's unfair. I like people, it's strangers that I object to living with me."

"Crap, Mother. You can't cope with visitors."

"I cope with you!"

"That's a tad different, Mother. Be honest, 'people' means you have to put on a face and be polite when really, you just want to be left alone."

She probably had a point. Most people think I am an extrovert. But that is an act, or rather a performance, that is part of me but not the real me. I have always liked cocooning myself at home. As long as I am surrounded by books, music and animals, I want for nothing more.

Peter argues that I have always supported him when he has played and sung in bands. I danced my socks off on nights out with friends. That is true. I always enjoyed myself once I was out, but deep down, I preferred solitude. And, as I've got older, I've needed it more. Having a stranger in the house puts my anxiety at level nine out of ten.

But I have to think of Pete and look again at the 'workaway' profiles to see if anyone catches my eye. The last probable candidate profile was of a shaven-headed young man, holding a freshly caught catfish.

"No, Pete, he looks like trouble. Definitely a non-starter."

"Well, the others won't suit either. I think we have to contact the catfish man."

"What's his name?"

"Roger. Apparently he wants a new experience. He has only been abroad once and that was a weekend in Paris."

"Okay," I said, "I'll email him but he looks like a thug and he is your problem if he causes trouble."

I rattled off an email asking why he felt we would suit him as a host for his first big trip abroad. His email arrived the following morning.

```
I'm scared of dogs and I
thought being on a farm would
help me get over that. I was
in foster care most of my
life. I'm a London Brixton
boy. I want an adventure as
I'm over 30. I have my first
passport ready to go.
```

"Pete, read this. What do I reply?"

"Well, he is being honest," said Pete, reading the email over my shoulder.

"I suppose that's a plus. But really, scared of dogs? What the hell happens when he meets Monty?"

"Monty and Lulu will be fine with him. Tell him to come," Peter said confidently.

Roger arrived on a big red sports motorbike. We met him in the town, and he followed us down the top track. But when he drove onto the bottom bumpy track, he pulled up.

"Don't think it will make it down this track, mate," he said to Peter. "This is a CBR600-FS!"

"No problem, Roger. You and I will push it slowly, avoiding the bumps," said Peter. "You drive down, Diane, and put Monty and Lulu away."

By the time I had parked the car, and secured Monty and Lulu in the house, Pete, Roger and the big red motorbike arrived at the front gate. Katy, Paz, Rita Mae and Martin were the welcoming party.

"I think you should meet the smaller dogs first, before we get your stuff inside," I said, hoping Katy wouldn't wipe her nose on his jeans.

"What do I do?" asked Roger.

"Walk in with Pete and ignore the dogs. Don't make eye contact with them." I instructed.

He shuffled in, and I wondered how Paz would react to a leather-jacket-wearing skinhead, who was already sweating profusely.

"Who's that one," he said pointing at a twirling Katy.

"She is Katy and has special needs."

Paz took over, recognising a London accent.

" 'ello mate, so you're Roger. Don't worry 'bout nuffing. Come in and 'ave a cuppa."

Roger was trying not to look at my little cockney girl who had sat down in front of him.

"This is Paz and she likes you. So that's one down," I told him.

Roger

"Diane, take the poor bloke inside and give him a drink," Peter said.

"Did you say the big dogs are inside?" Roger was stalling.

"Yes. Monty is inside. And Lulu. Lulu will be sleeping and, trust me, if Paz likes you, it will be okay. Monty is a kind dog."

Roger summoned his courage and followed me into the house, with the dogs and Katy trotting behind. I was plucking up courage to explain to this stranger that my dog was going to sniff his nether regions. Thank goodness Peter came to the rescue.

"Roger, the dog is going to sniff your balls then he will be fine."

Roger let out an odd sound, as he clamped eyes on my big boy.

"Mummy, what have we here?" said Monty, in his Prince Charles voice.

"This is Roger," I told him.

Monty shoved his nose in between poor Roger's legs, who automatically went up on tiptoes.

All I could do was smile at our guest. He must have thought he had entered a madhouse. He was probably working out how he could ride his motor bike out of the valley, without breaking it, let alone having the hounds of hell tear him apart. Monty stood back.

"Welcome. Do sit down and be aware of Katy. She has a nose problem," Monty told Roger.

I translated.

"He is fine with you. Come sit down. Have a drink then we will get your gear in."

Later, after a meal and a few tins of beer, Roger told us his story.

"I've only just got a passport and I went to Paris for a weekend. Then I thought it was time for an adventure."

"So why did you wait until your thirties to have a trip abroad? I mean, you are not married with kids," I said, not knowing if he was running from a wife and child maintenance.

"My favourite uncle died, my old fella died. I was hit by a Land Rover, all in the same year. So, that gave me the final push to get on with life. I have been working since I was sixteen, paying rent and taking care of myself."

Okay, so no wife and kids. I didn't like to ask more but the second glass of wine gave me courage. I also noticed the dogs were listening to Roger's story. Katy was being good so I felt she could stay up late too, as she was getting a little older. Martin sat next to Roger. It was past his bedtime but he was enjoying the new company.

"What about family?" I asked.

"Mum is still going, but that's another story. I

Roger

have two sisters, but we didn't always live together."

"Pee break," I said, thinking Roger would either carry on with his story or draw a line after we all relieved ourselves.

Martin followed Roger to the loo.

"Alright mate, you coming with me? That's good, 'cause a monster may get me," Roger said laughing.

I put some nibbles on the table, refilled glasses and waited.

"Yes, I had a funny old life when I was young," Roger continued. "The first day at little school, I was taken into care."

Pete and I put our drinks back onto the table. I didn't know how to respond. This young man was telling two strangers his life story, explaining who he was. We both leaned forward to listen.

"The school saw some stuff and called the authorities, or maybe they already knew home was difficult. Anyway, I went back and forth with Mum and Dad until I was twelve then I went back into the care system until I left at the age of sixteen. Then went into the world to work." He paused to take a sip of beer. "Now I'm here. So what's the work plan? I'm crap at getting up in the morning."

"Bloody hell, Rog, it's a farm!" Pete said. "In this heat we have to work early, then you can sleep all afternoon. Tomorrow we dig a trench for the new stable footings."

"Right, well, I best get some kip then," he said and staggered off to bed.

Martin positioned himself outside his door. I pulled his cushion close to him and told the little man, "Time to sleep, Martin."

He snuggled down and sunk into his usual deep slumber. Peter carried Katy to share the bed with Monty and Rita Mae.

The next few months were full of blood, sweat, tears and lots of laughter. Roger fought some demons and we fought frustration. One morning we woke to find a note on the fridge door.

I think I've drunk all your beer.

We looked outside and surrounding the garden chair was a mound of beer cans. Roger's bedroom door opened and Martin walked out. I glared.

"Martin stayed with me all night and then slept next to me," croaked Roger, who had obviously smoked too much. "Maybe I should leave. It's too hot and I'm tired."

Roger wasn't going anywhere. Martin felt he needed care so he was staying.

Roger

"Right Rog, let's start again. If you have a problem, let's just sit and talk, but we want you here."

Martin and Roger became firm friends. It was the first and only time our obsessive-compulsive-disorder dog chose to stay close to anyone other than us.

Roger and Peter

We introduced Roger to our friends, who loved him. He became my 'go-to' person for advice. Roger, like Martin, was special. Maybe it was because of his early life, or maybe it was because he was a naturally compassionate person. He remains one of our dearest friends.

When he finally left to continue his adventures in Portugal, we cried. Or rather we had 'dust in our eyes'. We waved until his red motorbike disappeared around a corner.

People come into your life unexpectedly and some have to leave, but the memories you make together remain forever.

18

Wilfs

Chari is dusting the curtain rails, while I sit on the side of Antonio's bed.

"Cleaning is an obsession with her. She can't help herself," Antonio says. He has been out of hospital for a couple of weeks, recuperating after his second operation.

"How are you feeling, Antonio?"

"I'm still tired, but it's all the medicine they have given me."

"How is your appetite?"

"Appetite!" Chari interjects. "He won't eat proper food. He just likes jelly sweets."

"You must get your strength back," I tell him.

"I want food but nothing makes me want to eat it."

I try to understand what he means.

"You just want sugar, is that it?"

"He wants a dummy with honey on it," Chari says.

The thought of Antonio sucking a pacifier amuses me. I realise Chari is frustrated that her husband will not eat the food she is cooking for him.

"You like chicken and rice," I suggest.

"How are all the animals?" he says, meaning the food subject is now closed.

We talk goat and Chari gets bored.

A week goes by. I am outside our house when Agustin phones me.

"Antonio is back in hospital."

"What's happened?"

"He had an epileptic fit and a high fever."

"Thank you for letting me know. I'll phone Nacho later. Do you need anything?"

"No, not yet. We will bring the goats back at the end of next month and I'll need a hand then."

"Okay, I'll see you then." I end the call.

Pete rushes out of the house when he hears me shout, "Shi—tt!"

"What the heck is the matter with you?"

"Antonio is back in hospital. Agustin says he had an epileptic fit. This is bad, Pete. This is really bad."

"Diane, we don't know the full details," Pete

says, and I know he is trying to placate me. "Agustin may have exaggerated."

"I don't think he was exaggerating. Epileptic fit is probably not an expression that's in his stoned vocabulary." My sarcasm hides my fear.

"We wait," Pete continues, ignoring my sarcasm. "We get on with things here until we get another call. I am sure the family will let us know if anything changes."

Two weeks later Antonio came home. I phoned him. El Maestro is resting in bed and enjoying taking phone calls.

"Antonio, Rigsby has got out of his saddle. Only for about ten minutes. Do you think the goats will be safe?"

"Diane, he will have made at least three girls pregnant," he says, laughing.

It is wonderful to hear him in good spirits. It has been a long road to recovery, since his last infection and operation, but today he sounds more like the old Antonio.

"The goats are coming back home soon and I have plans," he tells me.

"Let's hope Fernando did a good job and has fathered lots of kids," I say.

"We will know in a month's time, Diane."

"How are you feeling?" I ask, knowing he will lie.

"Me? Oh much stronger, Diane. They won't

let me visit the goats as everyone is scared of infection. But I'll be there when the herd is at Las Vicarias," he says quietly. "They won't be able to stop me."

I am assuming that, by 'they', he means the family. They, however, are doing what is best for him. But keeping him on bed-rest will not be an easy task. Deep down I know that keeping him inside, and away from his animals, will not help his recovery. But I'm sure his family will find a compromise. I swing the conversation back to my lovely old buck, Rigsby.

"He is not well, Antonio. His breathing has been bad all summer and nothing I give him has helped."

"Have you steamed him?"

"Yes, and given him two courses of antibiotics. But he is not improving."

"Well, that's it then. Getting out of his saddle and getting some goats pregnant is maybe his final goodbye."

I can hear his wife, in the background, saying soup is ready. I say my goodbyes with the promise that I will keep him updated on all the animal news.

I get ready to walk the girls downriver. For the past few days I have left Rigsby behind. But this upset him and his best friend, Isabelle. Izzy lost her adopted daughter, Pamela, who died suddenly, shocking us all. She and Rigsby became closer still and their friendship was wonderful to see. They ate next to each other, slept together and walked side by side. Although he was still eating, I had a feeling that I might lose him soon. I decide to video him that afternoon.

It is a beautiful afternoon and the walk is not too hot and not too strenuous. It gives Monty a chance to enjoy a more gentle walk. The big boy is feeling his age. He doesn't complain but he looks weary. His appetite is good, and his eyesight is still sharp. But he is old and I have to accept that.

Three hours pass quickly. We enter the corral and the girls dash for their feed. I notice Rigsby and Isabelle stay behind in the paddock. I grab feed tins and offer them to the two friends. Izzy greedily eats her supper but Rigsby refuses. I leave them to be together and head for the kitchen to rustle up food for the hungry humans.

It's 7 am, and I check the paddock. Isabelle is sitting next to Rigsby, who has died. Pete joins me and I am about to pay my respects when he holds me back.

"Wait," he says. "Look at the girls."

We watch as the goats, one by one, quietly walk up to Rigsby's body to pay their respects. We can hardly breathe as we witness a scene that both of us have only seen in a David Attenborough documentary about elephants. Isabelle does not move as the goats walk past.

"I'm not going to move him, Diane, until Isabelle walks away," says Peter. "She will tell me when it's time. Let them mourn."

※ ※ ※

Jonathan was growing fast. Yum Yum and Eugene were now big boys but they remained, as did Gracie, gentle with their friend. Jonathan had not been allowed to walk with the herd. I felt his front legs were not strong enough. The splint on his good leg had been removed and I had been assessing him every day. Before walking in the *campo* terrain, he needed to get his muscles stronger.

"We can't keep him in much longer, Diane," said Peter, cradling Jonathan in his arms. "He needs to learn about the outside world."

"Okay then, today is the day. But he will have to cross the river and that will be scary and difficult for him."

"I'll help him, like I did Mikki," Peter said.

"Right, but don't mollycoddle him too much. He has to work things out himself."

Peter was ignoring me. He was playing, *round and round the garden, like a teddy bear, one step two step and tickly under there*, finishing with scratching Jonathan under his front leg.

I was fighting a losing battle. Katy had moved away from playing football and taken up a much-needed post as 'ealth and Safety Officer. Peter needed another baby and Jonathan filled the gap. It was not one-sided. The stunning palomino-coloured boy adored Peter. It was Dad who comforted him when Mum stuck needles into him day after day. It was Dad who sung and rocked him. Hopefully, he would stick by Dad when we went for a walk, and would not be pushed around by the bigger goats.

Monty was on the case. He waited with Jonathan while the mad rush to leave the paddock settled down, then escorted him out and into the olive grove.

Jonathan loved his new freedom. He followed Gracie and together they munched on olives, herbs and different bushes. Philip and I took the goats across the river. There were enough rocks for the girls to cross over, leaping from one to another, without getting their hooves wet.

"Diane, Jonathan won't cross the river," Peter shouted.

"Where is Gracie?"

"She's across but he's scared. I'll go back and carry him."

"No, no. Wait. I'm coming."

Jonathan was frightened and began running up and down the river bank. Peter was now standing on a rock in the middle of the river, calling his boy.

"Peter, he has to do this on his own."

"He's scared, I'm going to get him." His fatherly instinct was in overdrive.

"Pete, come back on this side, I'm calling Monty."

Peter reluctantly obeyed and I called my trusty mastin.

"Monty, help Jonathan across. He's panicking."

He crossed the river and gently gave Jonathan the confidence to place one hoof on a rock. With Peter encouraging him, he made another step, then jumped across.

Over the next few months, Jonathan grew in confidence and strength. He knew which olive trees held his favourite gordal olives and stood underneath, waiting for Peter to pick them for him. Gordal olives are green and larger than the less fleshy, black ones. Jonathan played with Gracie, running up and down banks, enjoying life.

"He has an old soul, Diane. He knows stuff," Peter told me one evening.

"Do you mean like Chinni or Mikki?"

"Yes. I think he is here for a reason. Maybe it's

to learn what courage is and how we must never give up."

Everyone, be it human or animal, comes into our lives for a reason. The thing is to be able to understand what the reason is and what lessons we have to learn from them. As Monty says, "We have to stay alert."

Paz had taught Philip all there was to know about goats but Monty wanted to further his education. He decided to teach him about the dangers of wolves.

The late Johnny Morris gave voices to animals. Drawing on this and years of interacting with my dogs, enabled me to interpret the following conversation between them.

"Wilfs are very dangerous," said Monty.

"You mean wolves, Monts," chimed in Paz.

"That is what I said, wilfs."

"Ummm, Ummm, are they very big and scary animals?" Philip wanted to know.

"They are our relatives, Philip," Rita Mae explained.

"DISTANT!" said Monty. "Very distant."

Paz and Rita kept quiet. Monty continued.

"Wilfs are large creatures that live in the North

of this country. But some may have travelled down to this great valley."

"Umm, umm, what do I do if one comes here?" asked Philip.

"RUN!" Paz and Rita said in unison.

"Yes, that is correct. You run and tell me. Or inform any large canines that are in the vicinity."

"Umm… umm… and do I bark?"

"Well yes, you bark. And now that brings me to sky wilfs," said Monty.

"He means vultures, Philip," Paz explained. "Monty would often run up them big hills to attack them. Wouldn't you Monts?"

"Well, yes. Vultures are sky wilfs and must be attacked if they come near."

Rita Mae, wearing her lawyer's hat, asked, "Does 'attack' include all large flying creatures?"

"She 'as a point, Monty. There are different types of large flying birds," Paz stated.

"Sky wilfs are ugly buggers. You can't mistake them," said Monty.

"That is discrimination, Monty. Beauty is in the eye of the beholder," Rita Mae announced.

Martin got up from his bed and sat next to Philip.

"Eagles are also very big," he said, in his funny robotic voice.

"And beautiful," said Rita Mae.

"And majestic. Like you, Monty," said Paz.

"Umm, umm, now I am confused," said Philip.

Monty thought for a moment.

"Philip, my boy, sky wilfs are ugly beasts. Don't interrupt me, Rita." He held up a paw, silencing the family lawyer. "They watch the goats and babies, waiting for an accident. Eagles, on the other paw, are the Kings of Birds. They understand that I, Monty, am King of the Valley, while they are Kings of the Skies. We salute each other and mind our own businesses."

Philip still looked confused.

"I'll sum up, shall I?." said Paz. "If you see a big bugger flying in the valley, just give it a wave. If it's an eagle, it will wave back."

"Why are the dogs still awake?" said Pete, coming in from the stables. "Martin is usually flat out and Monty is normally snoring his head off by now. Rita, go in with Katy, I've just put her to bed."

"They have been explaining to Philip the difference between eagles and vultures."

Peter saw the new bottle of wine on the table.

"You must be two glasses in. Let's put some music on. We can sit outside, there is a full moon."

And so we topped our glasses and Pete put on the Bob Dylan album, *Modern Times*. We waltzed under the moon and stars to *When the deal goes down*.

19

El Maestro

Christmas had come and gone. The evenings were damp and cold. Pete and I were tucked up into bed, very early. Just as I was making a hot chocolate for us both, Chari phoned.

"Antonio is here, he is walking down the track. He made me stop the Land Rover and insisted on walking. Are you coming up?"

"Yes, I'm on my way," I told her.

I ran up our narrow path and met Chari outside his sheds.

"Is he not here yet?"

"No, he can't walk very fast," she said.

"I'll go and find him," I said and began to jog up the bumpy track. I was terrified, as one side of the track was a huge drop and it was almost dark.

"Antonio, where are you?" I called, but nothing came back. "ANTONIO!"

"Oh, hello," came a voice in the darkness.

"I can't see you."

He stepped out from a bush. I took a deep intake of breath. The medicine he was taking had puffed his face. He was leaning heavily on a walking stick, and walked towards me like a very old man.

"I've got to keep my muscles strong. I have to keep walking," he told me.

He didn't meet my eyes. He was looking ahead at the lights coming from his shed.

"Good idea. Come on, let's try not to trip up, you know how clumsy I am," I said, linking my arm in his.

"I have a plan, Diane."

"And what is your plan, Antonio?"

"I'm downsizing the herd and if Fernando has made half the herd pregnant, I will have a new breed that I can manage."

"Less goats, more milk, yes?"

"Yes. Fernando's breed won't need hours of hill work and I can buy lots of hay in the winter. I will be able to manage," he said.

"Brilliant idea. Now let's have a look at the new babies."

As we entered the sheds, Chari was trying to get a newborn kid to drink from its mother.

"Out of the way," said Antonio.

I anticipated his move. Quickly, I pulled out the padded beer crate to the correct position for him to sit and take over with the kids. His left arm wasn't very strong, nor was his eyesight, but his instinct was spot on. He manoeuvred the kid onto the teat and it latched on to drink.

"How did you do that? I've been trying for twenty minutes to get that kid to drink," said Chari.

"Patience and experience," he said. "Now, fetch any more that need help."

I watched as goats and babies were placed in front of him. He talked to all the goats, chatted and stroked the dogs. He was in his element.

"I'll say goodnight, then," I said to Antonio.

He didn't look up, maybe he hadn't heard. I slipped away to reheat the hot chocolate back at the farm.

"How is he, Diane?" asked Peter.

"He is still fighting, Pete," was all I could say.

Pete knew that because I was not analysing every moment of the hour I had spent at Antonio's sheds, I was extremely worried. A mug of tea and hot toast was needed. Comfort food, in the absence of chocolate cake.

"Remember when we first came over to look at property and we watched an old goatherder," Peter said, in an effort to shift my mood.

"Gosh, yes. We wondered what he was thinking about when he sat watching his herd."

"We came to the conclusion that he was either mulling over the meaning of life, or last night's football scores," Peter said, laughing.

"And a year later we found out what a goatherder really thinks about to pass the time," I said, and drifted off, remembering a conversation I had with Antonio one afternoon.

We had walked to one of his long green pieces of land that we had named Valencia. The goats had their heads down, eating the lush grass while Antonio and I ate lunch under the shade of an old olive tree.

"So Antonio, when you were on your own over the years, what did you think about?"

"What?"

"I mean, when you are sitting watching the goats, what are you thinking about?"

"Goats!" he said.

"Apart from goats, what do you think about when you get bored of thinking about goats?"

Antonio gave me a 'are you mad' look, because he would never get bored thinking about goats, but finally he understood what I was asking.

"I calculate how many olives are on a tree."

El Maestro

He saw my expression that this answer wasn't enough.

"I direct a cowboy movie, thinking of the best location to film," he said.

Now encouraged by my full attention, he found his stride.

"I dream about buying more land and work out goat paths all over Olvera. And, I would get rid of most of the olive groves."

"You would get rid of olives?"

"Yes. I would use the land to grow good vegetables and plant broad beans and wheat. I would turn the land back to how it used to be when I was a kid," he said, rolling a cigarette. "And get children back working in the *campo* and off their computers."

"You sound like you want to be a politician," I said, laughing.

"No, no. Politicians, they are corrupt!"

"You must get tired out, thinking of all that."

"Yes, it takes a lot of energy organising all that in my head," he said, tapping his temple.

We lapsed into silence for a few minutes.

"But this keeps me amused for a while," he said, grabbing his walking stick.

"What?"

He hung the stick on a low branch of the olive tree and sat, crossed-legged, in front of it.

"Watch," he said.

He swung the stick and dodged being hit on his head as it swung back towards him.

There was something very 'Zen' about observing a goatherder, dodging a swinging stick on a branch in the middle of nowhere.

∽∽ ∽∽ ∽

One of Antonio's favourite series on the television was 'Kung Fu'. Many times, on our walk back to the sheds on a spring evening, we would play 'take the pebble from my hand grasshopper'. Or sometimes we would play 'rice paper'.

While the goats were having their last half hour eating in the river bed, Antonio would smooth out a stretch of sand, before reciting a line from the Shaolin Master.

"When you can walk on the rice paper without tearing it, then your steps will not be heard," he said.

"It's sand, Antonio, not rice paper."

"Same thing, walk across don't make a mess of the sand," he instructed.

Carefully I walked across the sand, looked back and groaned. I left huge footprints.

"Once more," he said, and smoothed the sand over again.

I tried three times but with no luck. My prints were still messy and deep.

Then it was Antonio's turn. He took a few deep breaths and then crossed the sand like Kwai Chang Caine. When he looked back there was hardly a dent in the sand. He looked at me, grinned and repeated, "Then your steps will not be heard."

Antonio did not return to his goats' sheds again. I phoned his wife.

"He is very tired. And he only wants to eat jelly sweets again."

"Can I visit, Chari?"

"Yes, come, come," she said.

When I walked into his bedroom I could see Antonio on his side with his eyes tightly shut. Chari pulled up a chair for me and left the room.

"Hello, Maestro, it's me."

His eyes opened slowly, and he made an attempt to smile.

"I like to look at that," he said, his eyes drawing me to the bedside table.

I turned and saw a postcard that my friend Les had painted of a goat on a rock. I had given it to Antonio when he first came out of hospital. I could feel my throat closing up and tears filled my eyes.

"Are my animals okay, Diane?"

"They are good Antonio, they are good."
His eyes closed again.
"I like to sleep, sleep is good."
I stood and pulled the duvet up to his chin.
"You sleep, Antonio, I'll visit again soon."

He didn't answer and I walked out. I looked back at my friend only once.

As I drove back to the farm, I knew it was over.

That night, Agustin phoned to say that Antonio had had another seizure, and was back in hospital.

The following day we took the call. Antonio had passed.

It was a drizzly evening and we were getting ready to go to the gathering for Antonio, before the funeral the following day. Everything happens so quickly in Spain. We had barely digested the news.

Marilyn was close to giving birth, as was Ivy. Rigsby had managed to get these girls pregnant just before he died, as Antonio predicted. Before leaving, I ran to check on her one last time. My long suede boots had a hole in the sole and now were covered in straw. I tried to scrape it off before getting into the car.

"What do we do when we get there?" I asked Peter.

"No idea, just blend in I suppose," said Peter.

Blending in isn't easy when you are tall, English and blonde. We peered through the window, where inside, a great many people had gathered. I could hear Chari sobbing at the far end of the room. I clutched Peter's hand.

"Blend, Peter, blend."

We entered the gathering and heads turned.

"Blending isn't working," Peter muttered.

Antonio's brother came up to us, shook Peter's hand and gently put his hand on my shoulders. He guided us to the long queue of people lined up to pay their respects to Chari. We shuffled in the queue and as I watched people kneeling down in front of Chari to pay their respects, I panicked. If I knelt down, everyone would see the straw and hole on the underside of my boot. I relayed my fears to Peter.

"Of all the things to think about now," he hissed back to me.

I needn't have worried. Chari spotted us, shot up from her chair and ran into our arms. We three hugged and let the tears fall. Later, we found Agustin sitting outside, quietly weeping. We sat next to him.

"I can't go inside. Too many people. They

don't know him like us. He was like a father to me," said Agustin.

All we could do was nod. We sat together saying few words until Antonio's sister appeared.

"I thought I would find you all here," she smiled. "You loved him like family."

"I can't go inside, I can't," said Agustin.

"I understand. We will see you tomorrow at 11 am," she said.

"We will stay here with Agustin, if that's alright?" I said to her.

Her husband Nacho joined us. He put his arm around Agustin.

"We will all be together tomorrow, son, stay close to us," he told him.

The following day we climbed the steep road to the church. I was still numb. It hadn't quite sunk in that my friend had left this world. I was bewildered in Mass, as was Agustin. Peter had to hold him up at the end of the service. We made our way to the cemetery. It was there that it finally hit me. My legs began to shake as Antonio's coffin was placed in the niche.

"I can't do this, Peter."

"I think we have to stay until the end," he said.

"Can you do this, Pete?"

"No, I can't. I'll make our excuses to Nacho."

He told Nacho that we had to go, goat giving

birth, etc. I think he understood. He shook Peter's hand and gave me a big hug.

"Go to the farm, Diane. It will be alright."

As we closed the farm gates, we heard a cry from the goat shed. At top speed, we changed into our work clothes and dashed to see who had a problem. It was Ivy, she was in labour. Marilyn had already given birth.

"It's a girl, I'll put them in a pen. Looks like she has fed, so no worries with her," said Peter.

Ivy tried to push then stopped and cried.

"She has a problem, Pete, come and hold her. I have to go in."

"What's happening?" asked Peter, who was trying to soothe Ivy.

"Houston, we have a problem," I said, eyes closed.

I was working out how to adjust the baby that my neurotic girl was trying to deliver.

"How bad is the problem?" said Pete.

"It's a we-need-Antonio problem. It's Coco all over again." My anxiety level was going up to the penthouse suite.

I had to think. This was a bad breach and like Coco, there were no hind legs I could manoeuvre. I whispered under my breath, "Antonio, help me." I tried again.

"Visualise," he would tell me.

I began to talk out loud. Peter kept quiet. He knew why I needed to do this.

"I have to push the kid forward. Don't do anything, Ivy, just relax."

The contraction stopped for a few seconds, which allowed me to work right along the kid's back leg and gently, carefully, manoeuvre it backwards.

"Don't push, Ivy, don't push."

"Be careful not to tear the wall," Antonio would have told me. "Protect with a finger."

All the years of Antonio giving me a running commentary when he had problem births, came flooding back in that moment. I got one back leg in position and decided to pull.

"Push now, Ivy," I said.

She pushed and out popped a big girl. After I cleared her airways she cried loudly. I handed her to Ivy then bumped up her tummy. There was another baby who popped out easily. Both kids were fine and latched on to feed. We left both mums and babies to bond.

"You need a brandy?" asked Pete.

"I'll wash and sit for a bit. A glass of red would be great."

"You did good, Diane," he said.

I sat outside, wrapped in my big old drovers coat. I sipped my wine and let the tears roll down. Pete came and joined me.

"How will we manage without him, Pete?"

"We just have, Diane," he said. "It started today."

That night, we couldn't face sleep, and we couldn't face music, so we put on a DVD of Kung Fu. I listened to the Master's words and wrote them down. One day I'll frame them.

WHAT HAPPENS IN A MAN'S LIFE IS ALREADY WRITTEN. A MAN MUST MOVE THROUGH LIFE, AS HIS DESTINY WILLS.

El Maestro

20

Goats and Eagles

Chari told me the goats had been sold and asked me if I would I take on Manoli, Antonio's favourite.

"What about Bruce Lee?" I said. "Antonio said he would never leave Las Vicarias."

"Bruce has been badly injured, Diane. You had better come and see. The goats won't leave for another three weeks," she told me.

"We also have to sort the dogs out," I said.

"Yes, yes," she said. "Just come up."

I didn't want to enter his sheds. I couldn't face it, but Chari needed help. Antonio would expect me to sort out the dogs and his favourite goats. Chari guided me to a pen, where Bruce Lee had been placed.

"The young bucks beat him up, it's normal," she said. "His hip looks bad."

Bruce could barely stand. I got a small bowl of food for him, to see if I could persuade him to walk. Two steps and he fell down. Chari looked at me in despair.

"It's okay, Chari. We will move him when the goats leave. I'll make a special place for him."

"And Manoli?"

"Well, of course, she comes down too," I said. "Now, what about the dogs?" Chari started to cry. "I will take Rex. The farm down the road wants Bernado and Cheeta. People want India. I just don't know what to do."

"Chari, Cheeta comes to me. End of conversation. I'll talk to Jose about the other two small dogs. India goes nowhere. I'll find her a home. Do you understand? India is my problem."

India, Antonio's beautiful young collie, would not go to just anyone. He adored her. When he was ill he would always worry that she was being treated right. I needed the perfect home for her. I needed to talk to El Maestro.

I walked back down the path to the farm, stopping halfway to look at the view of the valley. I thought it was a good opportunity to have a chat with Antonio.

"Alright my friend, you have left me in a

muddle. So now you can help find a home for India. I can't perform miracles you know."

I searched the skies for some sort of sign, but in vain. Perhaps there was a time delay for such things? I carried on down the path and an idea flashed into my feeble brain. Put it on Facebook. All my friends are dog lovers, and they have all followed my mishaps/adventures over the years. Maybe someone can help?

That evening, I put up a photo of India that I had taken earlier that day and asked for help. A message came winging back from Ghislaine, who lives part-time in Olvera.

> Friends of mine are looking for a young dog. They are very experienced collie owners. They rescue mature collies but would love to have a young one this time. I'm phoning them now.

It was a perfect fit. Tony and Drew live in a wonderful area. Land, lakes and adventures with kind, caring people. I had no problem handing Antonio's precious girl over to them. She was now safe.

We had to re-shuffle the goats to accommodate Cheeta, Manoli and Bruce Lee. Ruby and Gerona were now together in the stable, next to the house. Chinni had died a month before. She died in my arms, it was her time. She closed her eyes and raced to the Rainbow Bridge. I also put Jonathan and Gracie in there. I didn't want to separate them from the main herd. It was safer for the little man to sleep, without the worry of getting knocked over by the bigger goats. Ivy's two girls were now being bottle-fed, because Ivy couldn't cope. The breach baby we named Jasmine but her nickname was Crash. The other had a problem. One back leg and hoof was deformed. I named her Shelagh and her disability did not hold her back in the slightest. She could bounce and play happily with her sister. My thinking was that Cheeta needed goats to take care of, and this mixture would be perfect.

The evenings were chilly. April is always a funny month. You may start the day in a jumper, by midday you're in a T-shirt, and by the evening a raincoat may be needed. It's a mixed bag. I had taken the goats out and kept close to home, as Monty, and Carmen, the sheep, looked tired. We had enough grazing around the farm to keep everyone happy. In fact, there was too much for the horses, and so they were locked in a smaller paddock at night to keep them from overgrazing.

Everyone had settled in their beds. Jonathan and Gracie were now used to sleeping in a different stable. Peter and I finished our supper and poured a glass of wine before discussing tomorrow's plans and catching up on the day's news.

"The horses are fat," Peter began.

"Hardy is big-boned," I said in defence of my old boy.

"Ruby and Gerona need a new salt lick," Peter said, writing a list.

"Monty was odd today."

"What do mean, odd?" asked Pete.

"He acted as if he had gone deaf or lost his marbles."

"Monty is not deaf, and he is as sharp as ever," Pete said. "He is getting old, Diane, you have to accept that fact."

"Yes, yes, but Pete, just before I called the goats in, he was standing and looking into the distance. And no, he hadn't spied a cow. He looked like he was in a world of his own," I said. "Then, when I called him, he ignored me. I called him five or six times before he turned and came to me."

"What was he like when he walked in?"

"Back to normal, tail wagging and asking for his dinner," I told him.

We both looked at Monty, who was fast asleep by the fire. He had eaten all his dinner and taken himself off to bed. He was now in a deep sleep.

"If he is still 'odd' tomorrow, we will take him

to the vet," Pete said. "Remember, I'm out early in the morning. If you are still worried, I'll make an appointment for the evening."

I slept well as we had a plan for my big boy. Peter left early in the morning. I had a lot to do on my own. The horses were fed first as Hardy was loudly kicking at the back gate, annoyed that his night grazing had been limited. I let the boys out and jogged back to quickly feed the dogs their breakfast. Monty wouldn't eat. It was the first time in his life that he had refused breakfast. I reached for my phone.

"Pete, make the appointment. Pop into the vet before you come home. Tell him it's urgent."

"Will do. I'll be home in around one and half hours, don't worry," he said, but he knew I was out of mind with worry.

I told myself to think logically. Maybe it's just constipation? We all have troubles when we get old.

"Come on Monty, let's you and me go for a little walk."

I left all the other dogs at home. I needed to have a one-on-one with my boy, to be able to observe him without distraction. I followed Monty out of the gate. He walked steadily towards the river. As he stood in the shallow water I faintly heard the words of Antonio, words he often told me. "They always head for the river, Diane, always."

Thirty minutes later, Monty died in my arms. His great heart had failed him.

Mine shattered into a million pieces.

"Diane, I need help," said Chari on a late-night phone call.

"Of course, what's wrong?" I said.

Understanding Chari on the phone is very difficult. I immediately put the call on speaker, so Peter could help me translate her fast and furious words.

"The farmer will put Bernado on a chain. He won't understand. Antonio would never let a dog be put on a chain. What do I do?"

"Chari, let me think and I'll phone you tomorrow."

She was satisfied with my answer and would await my call. She also told me that the goats would be leaving very soon.

"We can't take on Bernado, Diane. Don't make rash decisions."

"Who else will take him, Peter. Be honest."

We went back and forth until midnight. I opened a bottle of red.

"We are taking on Cheeta and she is pregnant.

We are taking Bruce Lee and Manoli. We have re-homed the other dogs. We can do no more. Plus, we haven't got the money to feed any more animals," Peter said.

I sat quietly sipping the cheap wine, wishing it was a large glass of Bailey's.

"What are you thinking, Diane?"

"I am thinking that Monty died at this time for us to be able to take Bernado."

"Are you kidding me?" said Peter.

"No, hear me out. It's all about timing. It was Monty's time, I know that. It would have been impossible to take on Bernado with Monts alive, impossible. Maybe the universe moves in ways we can't fathom."

Peter knew there no answer to that.

"What do we do, we have no money to get him 'fixed'?" he asked.

Peter had posed a reasonable question.

"Look, we take everything step by step. Let's get them down here and I'll talk to the ladies of Olvera. They will help with the vet bill, I know they will."

The 'ladies' are my English friends, who I try to meet up with for a coffee and a chat about anything, other than goats. They are all animal lovers. Also, they had followed Antonio's stories and were shocked and saddened by his death. The first thing that Bernado needed, was to have the 'snip'. I am a strong believer in neutering animals, which always caused arguments with Spanish friends, including Antonio. But that's the rule at Las Vicarias and I won't budge.

Our friends Jeff and Judy came for a visit a few days later. They love butterflies, and we have butterflies aplenty. We took the goats with us, watching and photographing beautiful butterflies of many colours and sizes. All was peaceful, until my phone chirped.

"The goats are going now, and crossing your land," said Chari. "I have Manoli and Bruce Lee in a pen. Cheeta and Bernado are locked up." The phone went dead and I leapt into action.

"Get the goats inside, now!" I shouted, probably too loudly, but I needed to change the gentle mood and get everyone moving fast.

Dogs and humans sprang into action. Peter automatically picked up Jonathan who was a tad indignant, as he wanted to be part of the stampede back to the corral. Just as the last goat entered the paddock and the gate closed, Antonio's herd walked across our field. Four men were helping move the goats. Jose, the new owner, bringing up the rear with the last two dogs of Antonio's that he agreed to take on.

Jeff immediately started to video this moment. Pete and I stood watching, unable to speak. This was it. Pete squeezed my hand, we were both blinking back tears. Finally, Pete spoke.

"Well, that's it. Diane, it's done."

Before I could answer, the phone rang.

"Manoli and Bruce Lee need picking up now, Diane," said Chari.

"We are on our way," I told her.

I grabbed two collars and leads, plus an old sheet.

"Jeff, Judy. Come on, we have to bring the goats down to the farm, and one of them needs help walking," I said.

My friends had come to us to enjoy the peace in our valley, and to photograph the wildlife, but now they were rushing up a path to move two old goats.

I slipped the collars onto both goats but quickly realised that Bruce couldn't walk more than a few steps before collapsing. I slipped the sheet underneath him, handing one side to Jeff and one to Pete. The sling would help lift him. Judy took Manoli, and began to lead her down the path. Jeff and Pete lifted Bruce Lee while I was at his head, encouraging him to try and walk.

Both men were now bent double, trying to lift the big old buck down our narrow path. Their backs were screaming, but Bruce had his head held high and seemed to be enjoying this adventure. His life this past year had been so difficult and painful. The young bucks had begun picking on him. He was the head of Antonio's herd, but he was old and weak. Antonio had not been there to protect him and to put him in a safe place to sleep. He had been attacked night after night. His hind leg had been damaged and he was not able to eat at the feeding trough. For Bruce Lee, any change to his life would be better than the one he had been living. I didn't know that this had been happening to him. If I had, I would have immediately removed him.

We finally arrived at the farm, sweating and cursing. I put the two goats in a small paddock by themselves and made up a small feed. Both looked at their bowls as if it were a full Christmas dinner and got stuck in.

"Drinks anyone?" I said.

"Oh, yes," our friends chorused back.

"Will Bruce make it?" asked Judy.

"He will live his best life. I'll get him as strong as possible, but he is an old boy. He needs to live in peace," I said.

Bruce Lee settled in well and enjoyed his meals on wheels. He was happy to share his residential care with Ruby and Gerona. I have kept my promise to Antonio. Bruce will never leave Las Vicarias.

When Jeff and Judy left, Pete and I walked up again to Antonio's sheds, armed with dog food and a collar and lead. Bernado was happy to see us, and tucked into his dinner, Cheeta ate, but her eyes never left the big front doors.

"She's waiting for the goats to come back," said Peter. How do we get her to come down to the farm?"

"We don't, it's too soon. If we take her down on a lead, she will run back here the first chance she gets. She needs to accept her goat family has gone."

"What do we do about Bernie, shall we leave him here with her?"

"No, we take him tonight. He has to have the 'snip' this week. It's best he gets used to his new life and anyway, Bruce Lee and Manoli will be happy he is there," I said.

Bernie settled in as easily as old Bruce Lee. We kept a careful eye on him to make sure he was safe with our goats. Jonathan walked up to him and introduced himself. That was the beginning of a wonderful friendship.

Pete spent time with Cheeta at Antonio's sheds. He took her breakfast and evening meal but more importantly, sat with her and tried to communicate what had happened. Three days had gone by and Cheeta had still not come down.

Bernie had his operation which went well, and he was recovering fast.

"She needs more time, Diane," said Peter, after he came down from feeding Cheeta her breakfast.

"I know, I know, but she is old and bloody pregnant. I need to really take care of her. She has to be comfortable and settled before she gives birth," I said.

Pete could see that I was working myself up into a giant rant, about everything that had happened this year. He also knew that the weight of responsibility resting on my shoulders was getting too much. I was close to cracking.

"Go for a walk, Diane, and go alone," he told me.

I snuck out of the gate, feeling guilty about not taking the dogs. But Pete was right, I needed some peace to get my head together. I needed advice. I messaged Roger and typed:

> I feel lost, Rog.

The shaven-headed Brixton boy, whose best friend was our little Martin, came back ten minutes later:

> He's gone Diane. You are now Queen of the valley. You can do this and if you need his help he will be right there at your shoulder. Stand tall mate,
> luv you.

Always the smooth talker. I walked back to the farm and for the first time in weeks, I had a big smile on my face.

"Feel better?" said Peter, handing me a mug of tea.

"Much better." I showed him Roger's message.

Philip started to bark, and Bernado joined in.

"Now what?" said Peter.

I dashed outside to see what had triggered the dogs and there at the gate, tail wagging, was Cheeta, very happy to be reunited with Bernado and the goats.

"Do you think she will go back up to the sheds again?" asked Pete.

"No, I don't think so. She knows her goats are gone. She will stay with our girls now."

I watched as Cheeta closed her eyes to sleep next to Manoli.

"Her heart must be broken. She needs time to process how much her life has changed," I said.

The following afternoon we took the goats out

with Bernado, Cheeta and Philip. Our girls were wary of Bernie, but content with walking with the noble Cheeta. They felt as safe as they did with Monty.

"Look at Jonathan," said Pete.

Pete's boy looked magnificent. His palomino coat shone and his white mane stood out.

"A prince," said Pete, proudly.

Against all odds, Jonathan was thriving. He loved Pete and walked next to him. Proud dad chatted to his boy all afternoon. We stopped to graze opposite Antonio's cliff. Cheeta walked forward to the river bed and stared at the corrals far above.

"Do you think she is going to cross and walk back up to the sheds?" Pete asked.

I held my breath, and then it happened. Cheeta sat, threw her head back and howled. My hand shot to my mouth. The dog was grieving. I looked at Peter, with tears running down my cheeks. Pete knew what to do. He stepped forward and sat next to her, as she continued to howl. Pete threw his head back and howled with her. The goats, Bernado and Philip stood still, listening to the cry from the heart of the great white dog, and the human who now joined her in her sorrow. We have learnt over the years not to comfort an animal in distress, but to be still, letting them work through their pain by giving calm, safe energy. This is what Peter was doing for her.

The goats started to slowly walk in the direction of home. Cheeta stood up and followed our girls. Pete and I exchanged looks, too emotional to speak.

It was that magical time of the evening, the moment when the valley turns red, then orange, then gold. Jonathan was bouncing alongside Peter. He stopped suddenly, and Philip began to bark.

"What is it Philip?" I asked.

"Umm, umm, sky wilf above us, Mama," he told me, looking up.

Pete and I followed Philip's gaze. The sky was now turning gold and there, soaring silently across the valley, was an imperial eagle. Cheeta sat quietly. She, too, was watching, hypnotised by the majestic bird flying above us.

Pete and I looked at each other, smiling.

We both waved.

Goats and Eagles

Antonio and his goats

Dedicated to the memory of

June Bell 3rd September 1955 – 8th August 2023
David Bell 2nd May 1952 – 12th December 2023

and

Antonio Pernia Zambrana 22nd February 1964 – 22nd March 2017

So, what happened next?

"It's over, Diane," said Peter, taking hold of my hand.

"It can't be, Pete," I said, tears filling my eyes. "She has always stood strong. She just needs a helping hand to hold her up."

"Sometimes you have to know when it's 'time'," Pete said, now standing in front of me to block my view of our wall.

I peered over his shoulder. I couldn't take it in. I know she was living on borrowed time. She was getting weaker every month that passed.

Peter poured a generous glass of wine and handed it to me. Taking a beer from the fridge for himself, I waited until he popped the seal until I took my first glug of the cheap red wine. We continued to stare at our wall behind the wood burner.

We had ignored the cracks and movement for a long time. There had been too many other problems on the farm to deal with.

The wall divides the old house from House Two, which we use as a store area. We had watched it, over the years, slowly bow and pull away from the outside wall. It needed to be taken down and rebuilt, but money and lack of manpower to help had put this major building work on the back burner.

"Okay. We need to think," I said, pouring another glass of red. To be fair, the first glass tasted like vinegar, and I was hoping my taste buds had adjusted enough to enjoy the second glass.

"Think about what, Diane?" said Pete as he eyed his emergency bottle of brandy. "We can't fix it at the moment and soon we will be living in a barn with the wood burner not in use."

I placed the brandy bottle on the table, realising that the bottle was old and nearly empty, but hoped the gesture would lift Pete's mood.

"What do we need, Pete? I mean what do we really need to live."

"One large room with a sound roof," he said.

"Like one of those container things," I offered.

"Yes, but we haven't got one of those standing in the olive grove, have we!"

So, what happened next?

"Right, point taken. We need a large area that a kitchen can be put in, a wood burner and all our books," I summed up.

We sat in silence and you could almost hear our combined brain cells whirling. The magic happened. In unison we both spoke.

"The milking parlour."

We grabbed our drinks and jogged across to the shed Peter had built years ago to milk our goats. Melanie and Wendy were inside deep in conversation. They were probably exchanging the latest antics of Janice, who was fast taking the position of herd bully.

"Excuse us, girls," I said. "We have come to view our new home."

They looked up for a few moments and then carried on chatting.

"It's just perfect," I said. "And we would have windows with glass.

Pete was on the opposite side of the shed, hands on hips.

"This would be perfect for the kitchen," he said. "Plumbing would be easy to sort."

The other goat, hearing our voices, decided to join us and trotted over to the milking shed. Pete now had a full audience, and he threw out man ideas for our 50-square-metre building. The goats looked impressed.

"Here, we knock a doorway through to the shower and bedroom," he told them.

I opened the window that looked out over the olive paddock. In the distance, I could see Antonio's sheds.

"How things have changed, Antonio," I said quietly.

Peter joined me with the girls following.

"He will still be supervising us," Peter said. "But at a distance."

I smiled. The valley was etched with my late friend's DNA. Whether he takes on the guise of an eagle or stands on the hill by his goat sheds, his spirit fills Las Vicarias.

I turned to address the goats.

"No, ladies, you have plenty of room in the other sheds. We are moving into this one. Any questions?"

Not one goat lifted a hoof. The problem had been solved.

So, what happened next?

Amazon Link: https://bit.ly/LadyGoatherd1

Amazon Link: https://bit.ly/LadyGoatherd2

A Request

Did you enjoy El Maestro: Lady Goatherder 2? If so, Diane would be forever grateful if you could hop over to Amazon, Goodreads or wherever you bought this book and scribble a review. It doesn't need to be long and you can rest assured, Diane reads and appreciates every one.

Amazon Link: https://bit.ly/LadyGoatherd2

About the Author

Diane Elliott was born in Kent but spent her adult life in Dorset. Although trained as a secretary, her dream was to work with horses. As an eight-year-old, she won many rosettes in horse competitions, particularly for the egg-and-spoon and musical sack races. Upon reflection, that was a good start for a budding goatherder.

Email: dianeelliott20@gmail.com
Photo Gallery: https://antpress.org/lady-goatherder-gallery/
Facebook Timeline: https://www.facebook.com/diane.eliott

Facebook Page: https://www.facebook.com/ExperienceOlvera

If you'd like to chat with Diane Elliott and other memoir authors and readers, do join We Love Memoirs. It's the friendliest group on Facebook.

https://www.facebook.com/groups/welovememoirs/

Acknowledgements

Ant Press for their professionalism and hand-holding, Victoria Twead for taking care of me, and the We Love Memoirs group for their kindness and laughter.

A big thank you to friends and family who have kept the faith and kept our sanity over the years. Anne Marie and Zoe Olvera Properties, Mateo and Family, Anne Crosskeys, Pat and Glen, Maria Del Mar, Paquito, Juan and family, Beth, Hayley, Julie, Daisy, Celia, Clare, Sue and Mel, Chari and Rosa Maria. The one and only Roger McGrath. Del and Karen over and above. My long-suffering family, Sandra, Amelia, Felicity, Rose, Arthur, Hazel and Elizabeth. And, of course, Peter, who is one in a million.

More Ant Press Books
AWESOME AUTHORS ~ AWESOME BOOKS

If you enjoyed this book, you may also enjoy these other Ant Press memoir authors. All titles are available in ebook, paperback, hardback and large print editions from **Amazon**.

These two booksellers offer FREE delivery worldwide.
Blackwells.co.uk and **Wordery.com**

More Stores
Waterstones (Europe delivery), **Booktopia** (Australia), **Barnes & Noble** (USA), and all good bookstores.

VICTORIA TWEAD
New York Times bestselling author
The Old Fools series

1. Chickens, Mules and Two Old Fools
2. Two Old Fools ~ Olé!
3. Two Old Fools on a Camel

4. Two Old Fools in Spain Again
5. Two Old Fools in Turmoil
6. Two Old Fools Down Under
7. Two Old Fools Fair Dinkum
8. One Young Fool in Dorset (Prequel)
9. One Young Fool in South Africa (Prequel)

- Dear Fran, Love Dulcie: Life and Death in the Hills and Hollows of Bygone Australia

PETER BARBER
Award-winning bestselling author
The Parthenon series

1. A Parthenon on our Roof
2. A Parthenon in Pefki
3. A Parthenon on our Roof Rack

- Musings from a Greek Village
- Musings from a Pandemic

BETH HASLAM
The Fat Dogs series

Fat Dogs and French Estates ~ Part I
Fat Dogs and French Estates ~ Part II
Fat Dogs and French Estates ~ Part III

Fat Dogs and French Estates ~ Part IV
Fat Dogs and French Estates ~ Part V
Fat Dogs and Welsh Estates ~ The Prequel

DIANE ELLIOTT
Lady Goatherder series

1. Butting Heads in Spain: Lady Goatherder 1
2. El Maestro: Lady Goatherder 2

EJ BAUER
The Someday Travels series

1. From Moulin Rouge to Gaudi's City
2. From Gaudi's City to Granada's Red Palace
3. From an Umbrian Farmhouse to Como's Quiet Shores

NICK ALBERT
Fresh Eggs and Dog Beds series

Fresh Eggs and Dog Beds: Living the Dream in Rural Ireland
Fresh Eggs and Dog Beds 2: Still Living the Dream in Rural Ireland
Fresh Eggs and Dog Beds 3: More Living the Dream in Rural Ireland

Fresh Eggs and Dog Beds 4: More Living the Dream in Rural Ireland

For more information about stockists, Ant Press titles or how to publish with Ant Press, please visit our website or contact us by email.

WEBSITE: www.antpress.org

EMAIL: admin@antpress.org

FACEBOOK: https://www.facebook.com/AntPress/

INSTAGRAM: https://instagram.com/publishwithantpress

Publish with Ant Press
AWESOME AUTHORS - AWESOME BOOKS

This book was formatted and produced by Ant Press.
Can we help you publish your book?

Website: www.antpress.org
Email: admin@antpress.com

Facebook: www.facebook.com/AntPress
Instagram:
www.instagram.com/publishwithantpress
Twitter: www.twitter.com/Ant_Press

www.ingramcontent.com/pod-product-compliance
Lightning Source LLC
Chambersburg PA
CBHW070502120526
44590CB00013B/721